S-6

ST. LUKE'S CHRISTIAN SCHOOL
13552 GOLDENWEST ST. 897-3074
WESTMINSTER, CA. 92683

# How To Grow Fruits And Berries

*Books by Lorelie Miller Mintz*

How to Grow Fruits and Berries
Vegetables in Patches and Pots
Threshold: Straightforward Answers to
    Teenagers' Questions about Sex
  (with Thomas Mintz M.D.)

# How To Grow Fruits And Berries

## LORELIE MILLER MINTZ
Illustrated by the author

Julian Messner  New York

*To my family,
may they always enjoy a sweet
and bountiful harvest*

---

Copyright © 1980 by Lorelie Miller Mintz
All rights reserved including the right of
reproduction in whole or in part in any form.
Published by Julian Messner, a Simon & Schuster
Division of Gulf & Western Corporation, Simon &
Schuster Building, 1230 Avenue of the Americas,
New York, N.Y. 10020.

JULIAN MESSNER and colophon are trademarks
of Simon & Schuster, registered in the U.S.
Patent and Trademark Office.

Manufactured in the United States of America

Design by Marjorie Zaum

Library of Congress Cataloging in Publication Data

Mintz, Lorie Miller.
   How to grow fruits and berries.

   Includes index.
   SUMMARY: Explains how to grow dwarf fruit trees and berry bushes indoors and outdoors, including information on where to buy them, materials needed, and how to plant, prune, and care for them.
   1. Fruit-culture—Juvenile literature.  2. Berries—Juvenile literature.  [1. Fruit culture.  2. Berries] I. Title.
SB357.2.M56         634         79-28753
ISBN 0-671-33086-1

# CONTENTS

Chapter

| | | |
|---|---|---|
| 1 | To My Readers | 6 |
| 2 | All About Fruits and Berries | 9 |
| 3 | Planting Fruits and Berries | 21 |
| 4 | The Living Tree | 32 |
| 5 | Fruits and Berries in Pots | 49 |
| | Guide to Growing Individual Fruits and Berries | 61 |
| | Where to Order Fruits and Berries | 90 |
| | Glossary | 91 |
| | Index | 94 |

## To My Readers

When I was a child, I eagerly awaited the arrival of spring. At the first whiff, I knew that summertime was just around the corner, and I would race to the market to see if the cherries had gotten there yet.

Even as an adult, I still believed that fruits and berries came from the market. Oh, of course, I knew they grew SOMEWHERE. But in a corner of my mind I supposed they grew in far away exotic orchards, tended by special experts trained in the secret art of making fruits and berries. So, that's where it began and ended for me—not in the garden, but at the market. And it wasn't until I was an old experienced hand at eating them, that I finally discovered the truth about fruits and berries.

My discovery took place on a very ordinary day, in an even more ordinary way, in the backyard of a friend's home. I hadn't really noticed anything special about that yard, and so I was somewhat surprised when my friend reached over to pluck a warm rosy peach from a nearby branch. Then she picked another, and then another, and another! Amazed, I began to notice in earnest just exactly what was going on in that small backyard.

Fruit was GROWING there! A swing hung from the branch of a tree—a heavily laden APPLE tree. The garage wall was covered in vines from which hung huge clusters of grapes and plump berries. And here and there were tiny trees showing the color of fruit between their branches. It was a well worn yard where balls and roller skates lay, and weeds scrambled for sunlit space. Not a far-away exotic orchard. No special experts. Certainly not a market. A backyard—just an ordinary yard.

And it was there the truth dawned on me. Was it possible that just the very ordinary sunshine, soil and water were all any fruit or berry ever asked for? Over the years, I found that in fact all this was true. Tucked behind city walls, happily growing in whatever nook or cranny I could find, fruits and berries did indeed belong with an eager amateur just like me. They became such sweet and long-time friends of the garden, I'd like to show you how you can have them, too.

L.M.M.

Putting down roots, a fruit tree or berry bush will bear loads and loads of mouth-watering fruit each year—for five years . . . ten years . . . twenty years . . . and more.

# 1 All About Fruits and Berries

Knowing all about fruits and berries used to mean just knowing how good they were, or knowing where to buy them. But now, knowing all about fruits and berries can mean having delicious fruit for your very own almost anytime you want. You simply grow them! Practically anywhere and in practically anything. All you need is a little space outdoors which is in the sunshine for at least six hours a day—and a liking for fruit.

Having a fruit tree or berry bush for your own is like keeping summer with you all winter long. And one of the nicest things about growing your own fruits and berries is that these summertime visitors become long-time, full-time friends.

Whether you want a barrelful of shiny red apples, bushels of golden peaches, or just a bowlful of berries for breakfast, space need not worry you. You do not need enough room for an orchard. Fruits and berries can grow in rows, in patches, along fences and walls, in tiny corners or anywhere out in the backyard. They can even be grown in pots (*See* Chapter 4) on rooftops, stairways, doorways, walkways, porches and patios. You can choose the kinds of fruit trees and berry bushes to fit whatever space you have.

If you dream of lying in a hammock under the shady green branches of your fruit tree, a *standard* size tree is for you. Every kind of fruit is available in such a size tree. Standard size trees usually grow over 25 feet tall and spread very far in all directions, needing lots and lots of outdoor space.

If, however, you dream of a whole orchard full of fruits, all of which are on your 12th story porch or in a tiny

Large or small

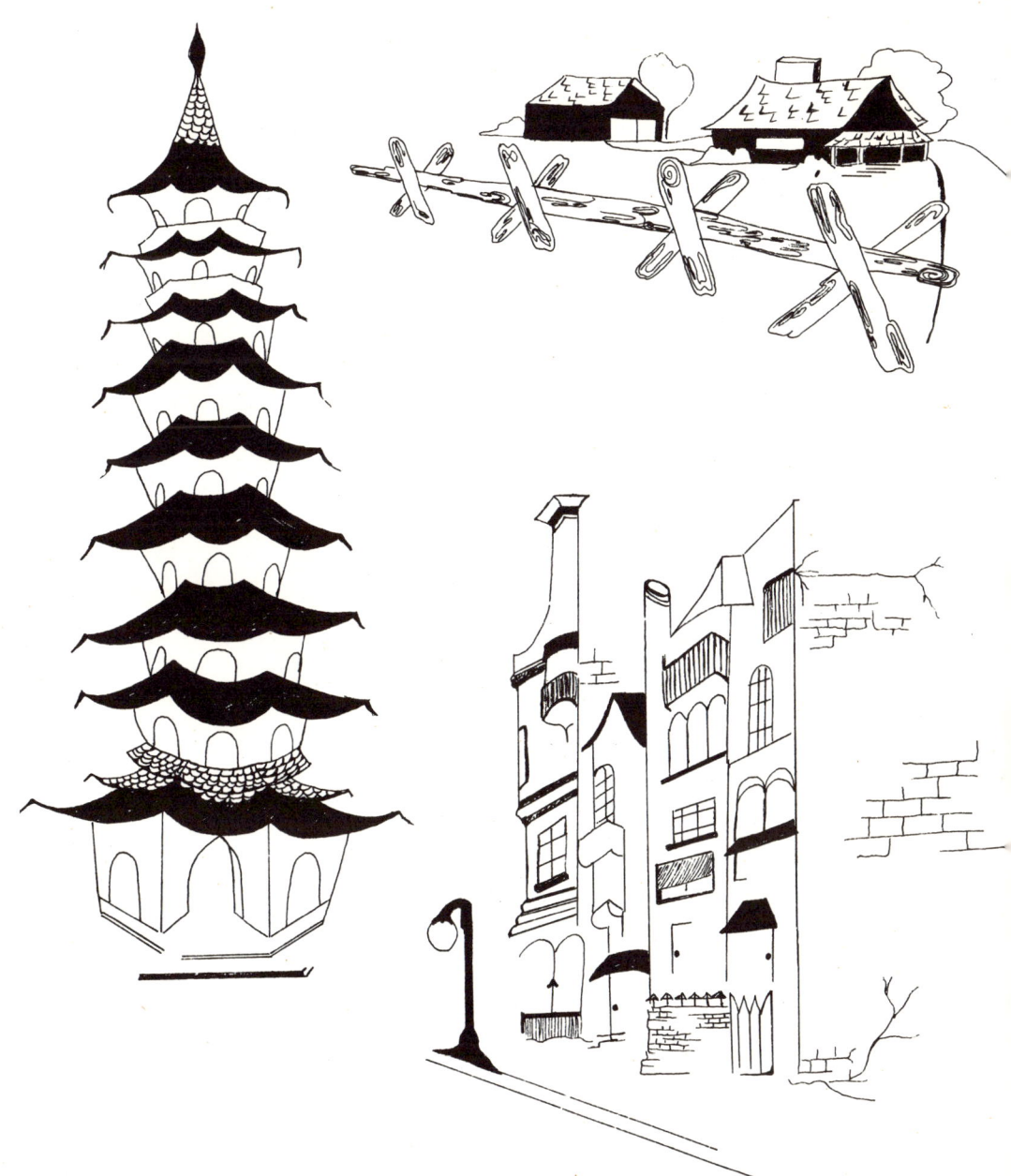

You can grow fruits and berries no matter where you live.

Luckily for those of us with big ideas but little space, most fruits are available in a dwarf variety.

garden size patch, then *dwarfs* are for you. No, not the Snow White Seven, but LITTLE trees, some barely three feet high, others growing only six or eight feet in height.

Although small in size, these mighty mites are giants when it comes to producing fruit. The fruit is the same size as fruit grown on standard size trees, and often the dwarfs produce it sooner. To give you an idea of the difference in size between dwarf and standard trees:

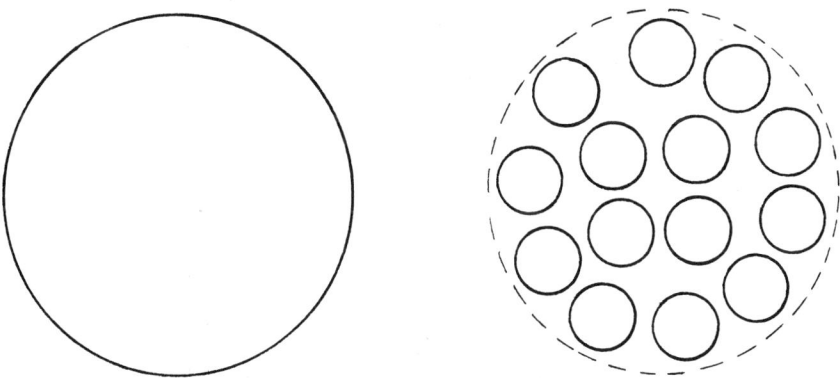

One large apple tree takes up the same amount of space as 12 to 16 dwarf apple trees.

Dwarf trees are either naturally short trees called *genetic dwarfs*, or man-made little trees just called *dwarfs*. Professional gardeners make regular *dwarfs* through a process called *grafting*.

Grafting is done by cutting off the top of one type of tree and bandaging it to the bottom of another type of tree. These two bandaged pieces soon heal and grow together to form a whole new tree, a much smaller variety of fruit tree. The bottom portion of the tree is the *rootstock* which goes underground. The top part is the fruit-producing portion of the tree.

*All About Fruits and Berries* · 13

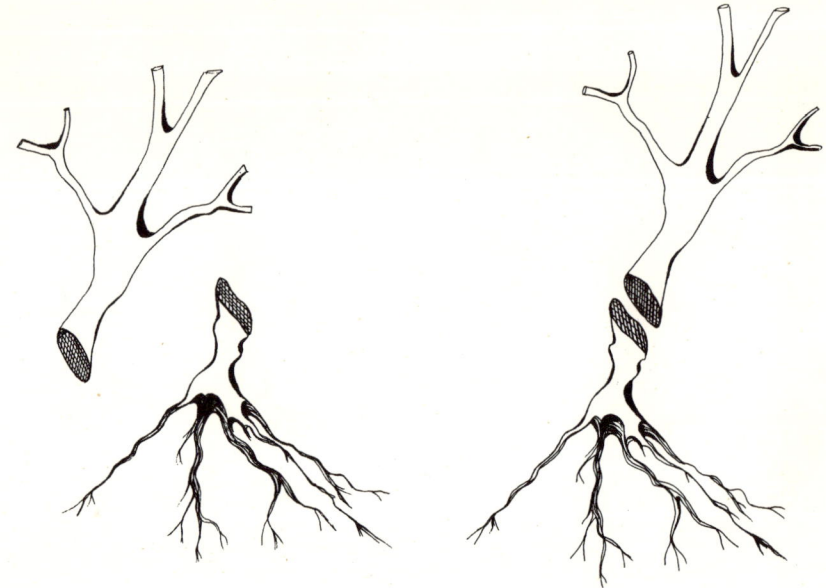

Man-made dwarf trees are actually small trees made up of pieces of two different trees.

The rootstock keeps the tree small because it originally came from a very small type of tree. The top portion produces the type of fruit desired. When the graft heals, the tree looks entirely whole. The only noticeable thing is a small bump where the two parts were joined together. This bump, called the *bud union*, must always be kept above the level of the soil. If it touches the soil, the tree might begin putting down new, large size roots and develop into a large size fruit tree.

Dwarf trees are available in most nurseries. Some are tiny dwarfs barely three feet high, other dwarfs grow to six feet tall. Semi-dwarf trees grow a bit larger, perhaps

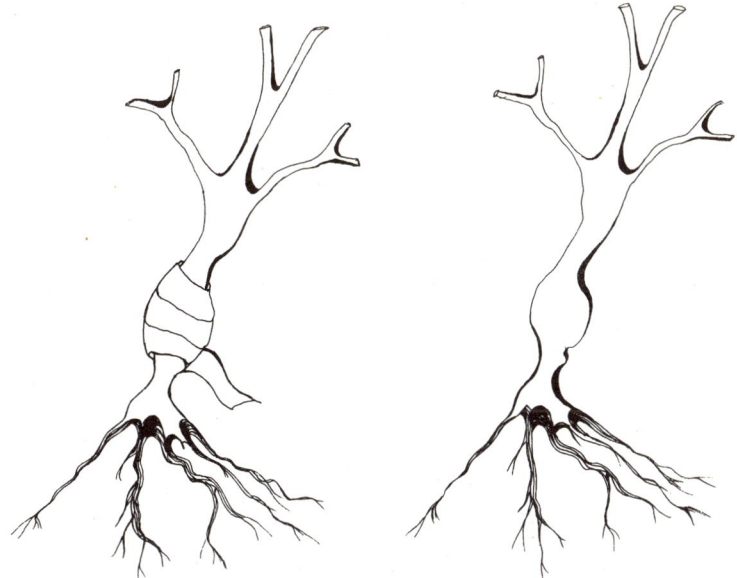

Bud union

eight to ten feet tall.

    Most fruits are available in different varieties suited to growth in all kinds of climates. However, because some fruits need *cold* winters while others need *warm* winters, you should check with your local nursery people before buying the tree. They will help you choose a variety of fruit tree that will do best in your particular climate. Local nurseries usually carry the varieties best suited for growing in their particular area. If they don't stock what you want, they will order it for you.

    Climate is, therefore, one consideration. It may influence your decision on when to plant fruit trees and berry

*All About Fruits and Berries* · 15

bushes outdoors, but it will not keep you from growing fruit trees at all. For by growing the smaller dwarf types, you don't have to depend completely upon outdoor climate.

If you want to grow a certain kind of fruit that is not supposed to do well in your area, you might try to do it anyway. Just do it in a pot! This allows you to bring your dwarf potted fruits indoors during the cold winters, and gives you more freedom of choice in deciding what to plant. A tropical pineapple orchard may be unheard of in the cold northern plains, but a potted tropical tree that can spend winters inside with you, near a sunny window, might be a wonderful idea!

So, consider the climate, remember the pot, then make your choices!

The last point to think about is an important one. Can your tree make fruit all by itself? Probably not. Most fruit trees are *self-sterile*. The word *sterile* means being unable to produce fruit. Self-sterile is a natural condition of many fruit trees in which the same variety trees, though having male and female parts, cannot fertilize each other to produce fruit. In order to bear fruit, the blossoms on your fruit tree will need to be fertilized by pollen from the blossoms of a slightly *different* variety of tree. (Pollen is a powderlike substance produced in the blossoms.)

This process is called *pollinization*, and your tree will need to be *pollinated* in order to make it fertile. In the case of a tree, being fertile is the ability to bear fruit. Your tree

Start with the idea that anything is possible. It may be freezing outside, but it can be summertime inside with you and your tropical baby!

will need a companion tree planted nearby to act as a pollinator.

REMEMBER, THE COMPANION TREE MUST BE THE *SAME TYPE* OF FRUIT TREE, BUT OF A SLIGHTLY *DIFFERENT VARIETY* OF THAT TYPE OF TREE. AND IT MUST BLOSSOM AT THE SAME TIME OF YEAR. A *variety* is any plant of a certain kind which differs only slightly from others of that kind. For example, Alberta peaches are slightly different from a variety called Freestone. Both are peach trees, but of different varieties.

Some trees are *self-fertile*. These trees are able to produce fruit all by themselves. But they, too, will produce more fruit when planted close by a companion tree.

Your part in the pollination process is quite simple. All you need do is to ask the nursery salesperson what variety to plant along with your tree to act as a pollinator, then simply plant them both! Either plant them about ten feet apart if you have the space, or plant them both together in the same hole about one or two feet apart.

The reason pollinating is so easy is because Mother Nature has given fruit trees a very special method of pollination: blossoms on the tree and a bee on the wing. Bees, which are dependent upon the blossoms for nectar, pollinate the trees. They fly back and forth between trees, and in the process brush up against the pollen of the blossoms. While carrying on their body hair the different varieties of pollen necessary for fertilization, the bees transfer the pollen as they fly from one blossom to another in their search for nectar. In this way, they pollinate the tree.

To pollinate fruit trees, all you need do is provide two varieties of trees. Spring will provide the blossoms and the bees.

Before you plant, you will need to gather together the following materials:

Stakes—one six-foot wood stake for each tree or berry bush

Wire or rope—for berry bush support

Tree tape—plastic tape for tying trees to stakes

Planter mix—a two-cubic-foot bag for every two trees that will be planted in the ground, or

Potting soil—a two-cubic-foot bag for each two trees that will be planted in pots.

Citrus food

Pruning shears

Insecticide—"Rotonone"

A hose

A shovel

Gardening gloves

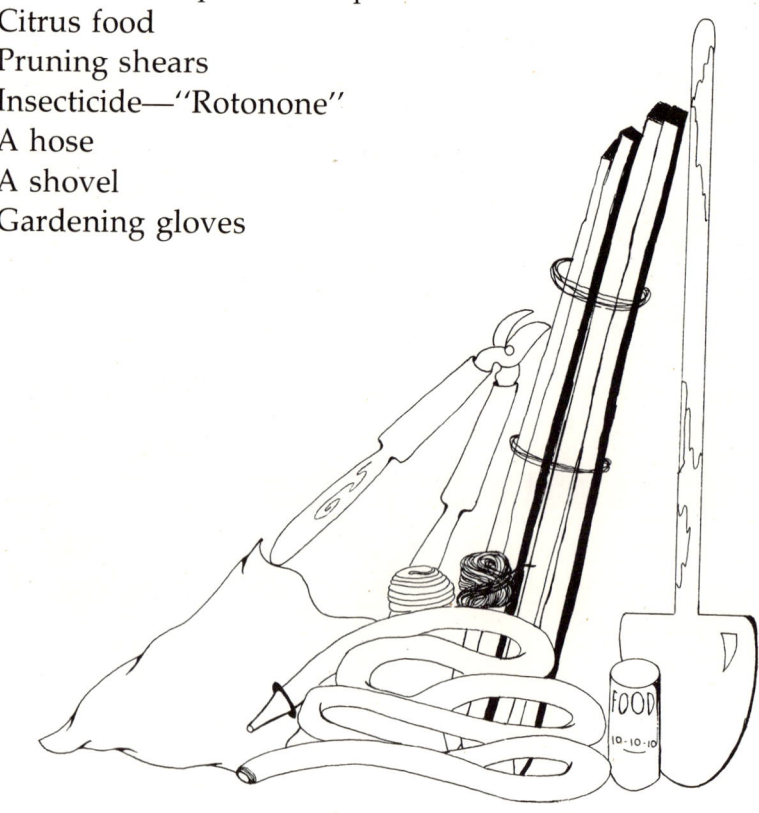

# 2 Planting Fruits and Berries

When you buy a fruit tree, it will usually be about one or two years old. It will not yet have borne fruit. It will be very spindly, have just a few wispy bare branches, and roots at one end. A berry bush will also be about a year old, and will look like a twig with roots.

With the exception of *citrus* fruits which keep their leaves all year, all fruit trees and berry bushes lose their leaves each year. During the winter, they are in a *dormant* period. The following spring they will bloom once again.

ALL FRUIT TREES AND BERRY BUSHES SHOULD BE PLANTED WHILE IN THEIR LEAFLESS, DORMANT STATE. IN MILD CLIMATES, PLANT IN VERY LATE WINTER. IN COLD CLIMATES, PLANT IN EARLY SPRING WHEN THE GROUND THAWS.

Trees and berries can be purchased from a local nursery or even through a mail-order catalog from a nursery located out of your area. Most plants are usually available in nurseries in bare-root form, at the right time for planting.

### BARE-ROOT TREES

The bare-root season arrives in late winter or early spring. Bare-root means exactly what it sounds like. The roots of the trees and bushes sold this way are bare with very little soil clinging to them. The trees and bushes are stored in large sawdust bins at nurseries. Fruit trees and berry bushes sold bare-root have not yet borne fruit, and it will take usually one, perhaps two, seasons before they are mature enough to bear fruit.

Before you buy bare-root fruit trees or berry bushes, you will need to prepare the soil a few days ahead of time. Roots need soil—fast. Always plant bare-root trees and bushes the same day you bring them home.

Be sure to keep the roots *damp* until you get your tree home.

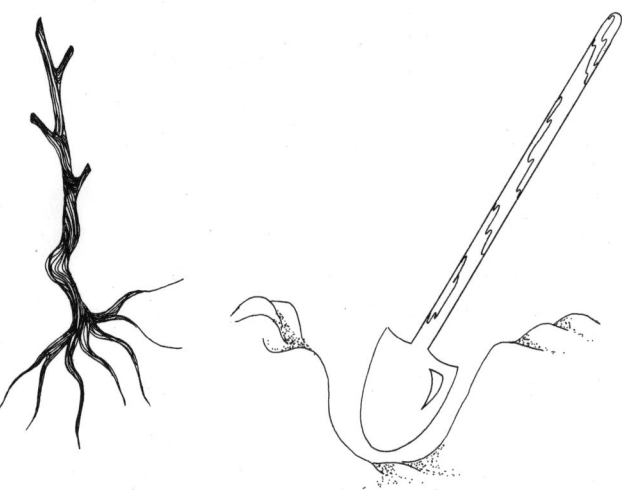

Bare-root trees and berries must be planted right away.

## CANNED TREES AND BUSHES

Fruit trees and berry bushes are also available in a temporary container filled with soil—a nursery store can. These containers usually house older trees, most of which have already borne fruit. Citrus trees are always sold in cans, no matter what their age. Buying a "canned" fruit tree or berry bush is a way of getting a tree which will bear fruit much faster. However, it is much more expensive to buy that way.

When buying canned trees, always look for shiny new green leaves. Good, healthy plants look fresh and vigorous. Dried up, tired and sick plants always look dried up, tired, wilted and limp—sick.

Canned trees can wait to be planted. Place them in a sunny spot, away from too much wind, and just remember to water them about three times a week.

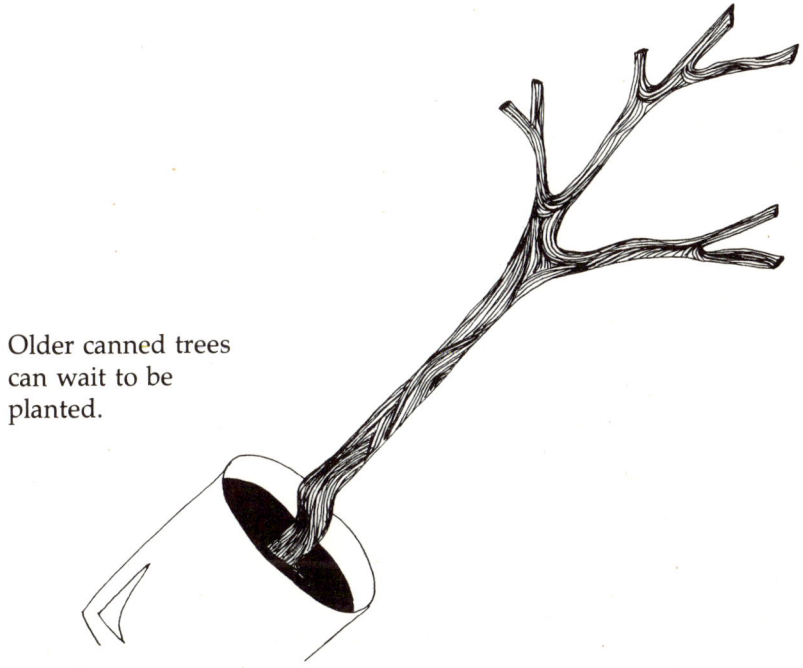

Older canned trees can wait to be planted.

## PLANTING FRUIT TREES

As the place you choose to plant your fruit tree or berry bush will be its permanent home, make sure to improve the soil by adding planter mix before you do your planting. This will provide your tree with the kind of home it will always want to live in. GOOD SOIL IS THE HEART OF GOOD GARDENING. Your soil will need to be soft and crumbly, not hard packed clay, nor dry sifted sand.

*Plant standard size trees 15 feet or more apart.*
*Plant semi-dwarf six to eight feet apart.*
*Plant very small dwarfs four feet apart.*

1. *Bare-root tree.* Dig a hole 18 inches deep and twice as wide as the roots when they are spread out.
   *Canned tree.* Dig a hole twice as deep and twice as wide as the container.
2. Mix the soil from the hole with an equal amount of planter mix.

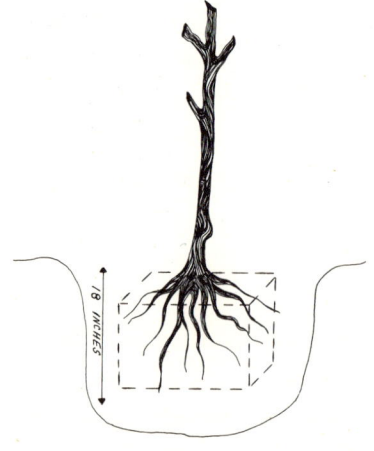

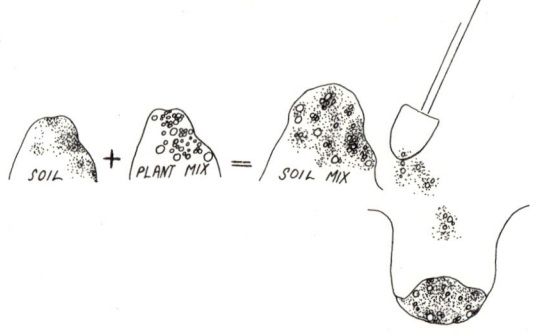

3. Shovel enough of this mixture back into the hole, so that about half the hole is filled.
4. Remove the tree from the container if it is a canned tree. (To remove the tree, cut the can with pruning shears.) Place the tree into the hole. Spread the roots of the tree over the soil if it is a bare-root tree.
5. Fill in the remaining soil mixture around the roots. Press soil firm as you work.
6. The soil mixture should come up to the same level of the tree trunk as it did in the original container.
7. Press the soil down firmly all around the base of the tree, with your hands, or step on it firmly. Turn the hose on low and let the water run slowly at the base of the tree. Then press the soil down again.

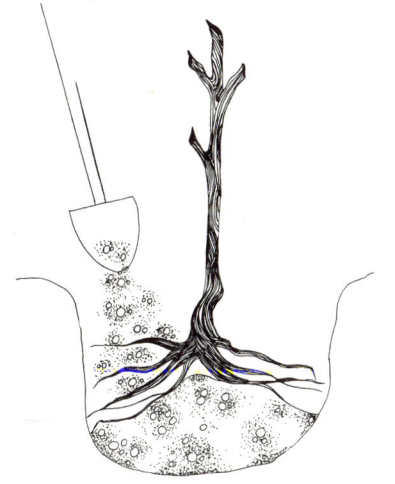

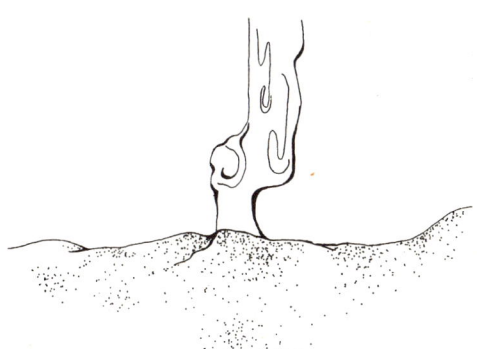

Always keep the bud union two inches above the level of the soil.

*Planting Fruits and Berries* · 25

Use the left over soil to form an earth ring about two feet away from the trunk of the tree. This earth ring will create a basin, allowing water to collect at the base of the tree and soak down to the deeper root zones underground.

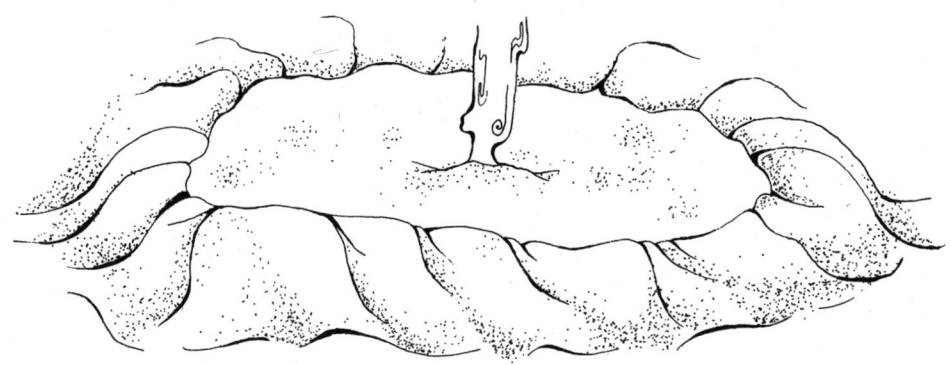

### AFTER PLANTING

Immediately after planting, you will have to cut back the branches of your tree. This is called *pruning*. The aim of pruning is to insure good fruit production. (For more information about pruning, *see* Chapter 3.)

If your tree looks like a stick with two or three very tiny stubs for branches, it has already been pruned, and you will not have to do so again until next year. If your tree has many long thin whip-like branches, it must be pruned *now*.

1. Cut a few inches off the top of the tree.
2. Choose three of the sturdiest looking branches which are spaced about six inches apart and are evenly distributed all around the trunk. Cut all other branches off—cleanly at the trunk.
3. Cut the three branches back to four inch stubs.
4. Place a stake about two inches away from the tree trunk so it will not rub against the trunk. Hammer the stake one foot deep into the soil. Tie your tree to the stake, using plastic tree tape. Finally, water again, letting water fill to the top of the earth ring basin.

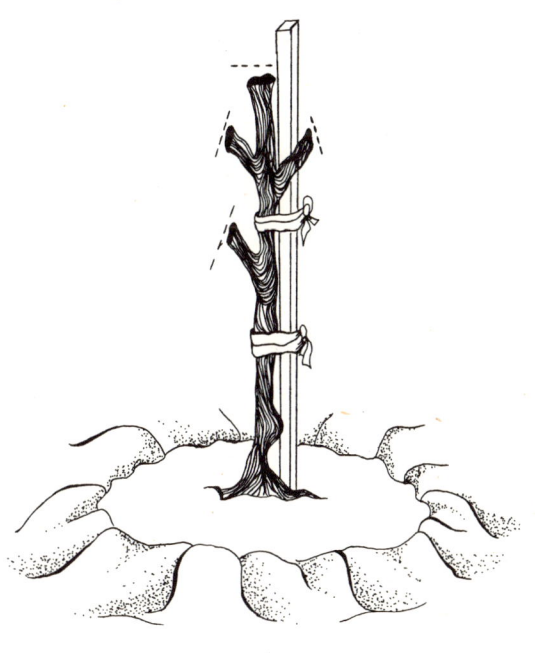

## PLANTING BERRY BUSHES

Berries are divided into three groups.

*Bushes:*

These are small bushes with lots of stiff branches

*Planting Fruits and Berries · 27*

which do not need any support to stand up straight.
*Canes:*
    Cane fruits make up the group which are often referred to in fairy tales—those famous bramble and briar patches we all remember from Peter Rabbit and Sleeping Beauty. Some of the stalks and branches, called canes, have thorns. The berries grow on these long thin *canes*. The canes are not strong and bend easily. They must be supported upon wires (or heavy string) and stakes. If berry canes are not tied onto these supports, they will bend over and tangle on the ground, forming a thick thorny briar patch not even Prince Charming could get through!
*Vines:*
    Vines are longer and softer than canes and have no thorns. Grapes grow on vines.

## TO PLANT

Berries are planted very much like trees except closer together. Plant berries two to three feet apart in rows. The rows should be three feet apart.
1. Bare-root berries: Dig a hole twice as wide and twice as deep as the roots when they are spread.
   Canned berries: Dig a hole twice the size of the container.
2. Mix the soil which you have removed from the hole with an equal amount of planter mix.
3. Fill at least half the hole with this mixture.

4. Remove the berry bush from its can, if it is a container plant, and place it in the hole. If your berry bush is a bare-root bush, fill in a bit more of the soil mixture in the hole and carefully spread the roots of the bare-root berry bush over the soil.
5. Fill in the remaining mixture and press in place. Water for about five minutes and press firmly once again. Make sure your plants are at the same level in the soil as they were in the container. Do not bury too much of the stem. Cut the bush back to a six-inch stub above the ground and finally, water again.

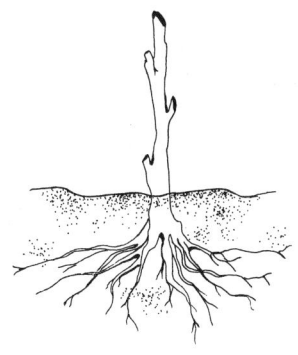

Proper planting depth for berry bushes.

## AFTER PLANTING

Before the bushes really need it, is a good time to provide a support system for your berries. If you plant berries along a wall, you can use the wall for support. You will need four large nails. Hammer one nail at each end of a wall 18 inches above the ground. Hammer another set of nails 18 inches above the first set. String wire or rope

*Planting Fruits and Berries · 29*

across the wall from one nail to the other. As your berry bushes grow, these two berry lines will support the canes.

If you have a fence, you simply tie the berries to it as they grow. If you have no fence or wall, you can provide support in either of two ways:

*Tepee style.* After pruning your berry vines, pull them together at the top and tie with a strong string or wire. The vines will support each other this way.

*With stakes and wire.* Hammer a stake two feet into the ground at each end of a row. String wire from one stake to the other at a height of 18 inches above the ground. String a second wire 18 inches above the first wire. This will allow you to train your berries to behave.

Teepee style.

Wire and stake support system.

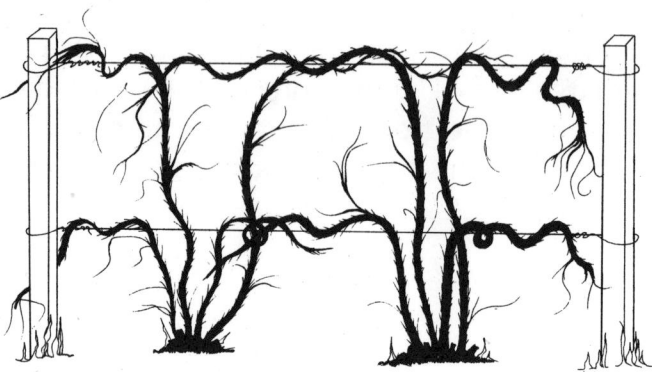

Now—all you need is patience.

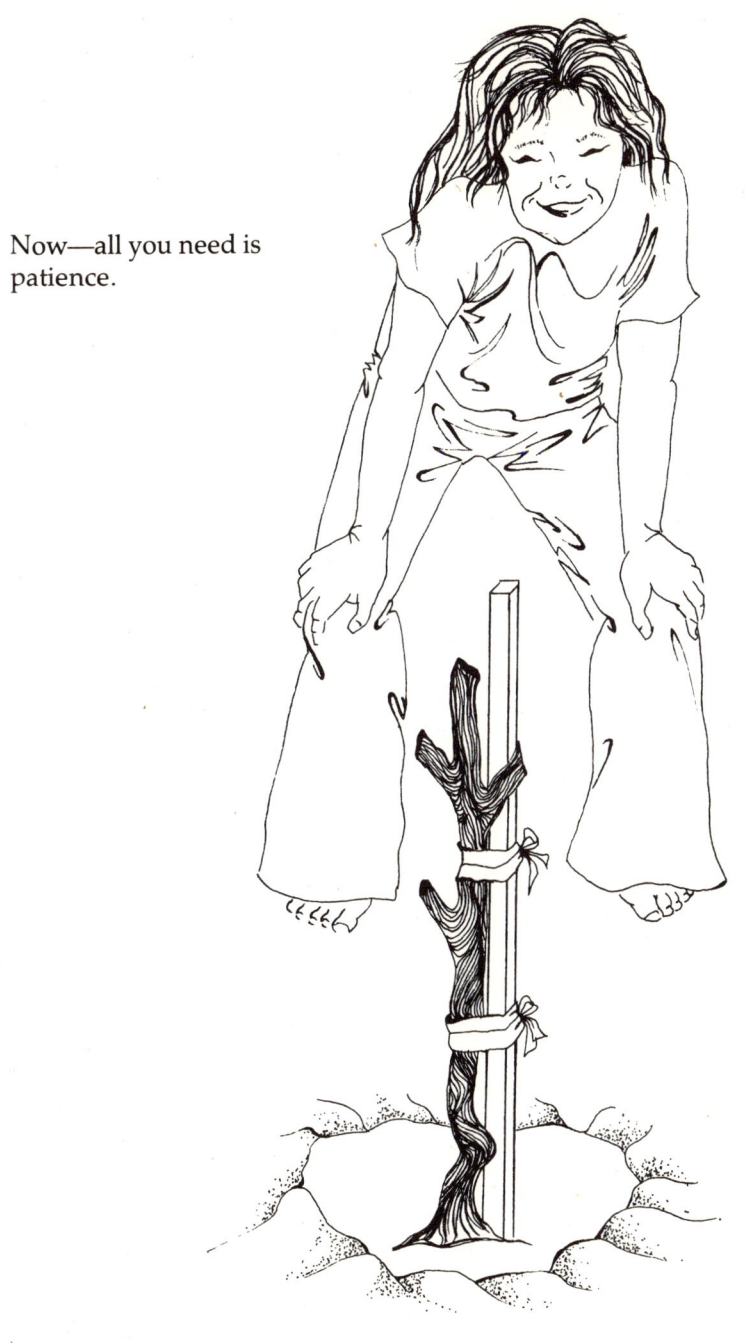

# 3  The Living Tree

Planting your fruit trees and berry bushes is only the beginning. Soon after planting, they will begin to change dramatically. From bare looking little twigs into tiny trees bursting with fragrant blossoms each year, fruit trees and berry bushes make spring really come true. Watching your own private springtime is exciting and rewarding. And it is an especially important time, for what you will be doing now is to ensure loads and loads of great fruit later on.

## SPRING AND SUMMER

*How To Water Newly Planted Trees*

Water your trees deeply, for trees like *irrigation*, not sprinkling. Test when your trees need water by looking underground. New trees need to be watered when the first two inches of topsoil become dry. Dig up a little soil with a spoon to check those top few inches. During the first few months, watering is usually necessary at least once a week.

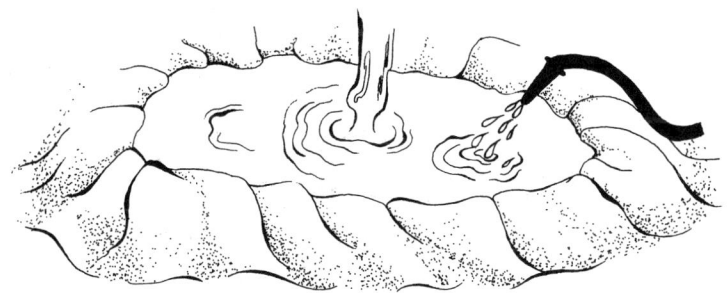

Place a hose inside the earth ring at the base of the tree and let the basin slowly fill with water. DO NOT LET THE WATER OVERFLOW THE RIM OF THE EARTH RING.

*How To Water Older Trees*

Every two weeks, dig up a small shovelful of soil near the trunk. When the soil is squeezed into a ball, it should cling together loosely. It should not form a soggy wet clump, nor sift through your fingers fine and dry as dust. Replace the test shovelful and press soil firmly back into place.

To water, lay a hose inside the earth ring around the tree and fill with water, but do not overflow. This slow watering will take about two hours and should be done every few weeks. To test watering depth, use a stiff wire. The wire will only penetrate where the soil is wet. You should be able to push the wire into the soil to a depth of about one to two feet for dwarf trees and three feet for standard size trees.

*How To Water Berry Bushes*

Allow the hose to run slowly between the rows of berry bushes until the water has soaked into six or more inches of soil. Push a stiff wire into the soil to see how far down the water is soaked. The wire will only penetrate easily where the soil is wet. Check the soil condition by digging up a small amount of soil each week with a spoon or the tip of the shovel. Water twice or three times a week during hot weather, less often if weather is cool or damp.

*Mulch*

This is a kind of material with which you cover the ground around and in between your fruit trees and berry bushes. Berry bushes especially like mulching. Mulch can be purchased either at a nursery store or a lumber yard, or even found in your garden, or your living room. Mulch material can be:

| | |
|---|---|
| Sawdust | Dried out grass clippings |
| Woodshavings | Old newspapers |
| Redwood bark | Hay |
| Black plastic sheets | |

These materials help keep the temperature of the soil even. In very hot weather, mulch keeps the soil cool and prevents harsh drying. In very cold weather, alternating freezing and warm temperatures cause the soil to lift, uprooting shallow roots. Mulch prevents this. Mulch also keeps fruits and berries from touching the soil and rotting, and smothers weeds!

*To Mulch Berries:* Lay a two-inch layer of mulch around your berry bush four weeks after planting.

*To Mulch Trees:* Lay a two-inch layer of mulch under branches. Keep mulch one to two feet away from tree trunks.

### HOW TO FEED TREES AND BERRY BUSHES

Mother Nature does a marvelous job of manufacturing food for fruits and berries. Each piece of fruit has anywhere from 30 to 50 leaves working for it. Leaves make the sugar which fruits need by using *carbon dioxide*, *water* and *sunlight*. Sometimes they need a little help from you in the way of plant food. When the leaves on your tree or bush look yellow, they are asking for food. Abundant green leaves mean your plant's diet is in good shape.

Plant food for fruits and berries is called citrus food, or sometimes citrus fertilizer. All brands will have three numbers on the label. The numbers may vary slightly from brand to brand. These three numbers refer to the amount of minerals called *nitrogen*, *phosphorous*, and *potassium* which the plant food contains. Nitrogen keeps leaves green. Phosphorous and potassium ensures healthy root systems. Your nursery will be able to recommend a good plant food.

In the first year, feed your plants during June or early July. Each year thereafter, feed twice—once when spring begins, around March, and again in June before the fruit is fully ripe. The roots fan out, just like the branches, so scatter the food *away* from the tree trunk, *under the branches*, where the food can soak down to the roots. Water your fruit trees and berry bushes deeply after each feeding to help the food get down through the soil to the roots.

The first season you will have lots of lush green growth—but probably no fruit. Then finally, perhaps during the second season, on one exciting summer day, there it will be—your first fruit! Tiny at first, but unmistakably signaling bigger and better things to come, your tree will have finally done it. And at that proud moment, it will seem to you as if no other tree has ever done the same, and certainly never so well.

### *HOW TO PROTECT YOUR FRUITS AND BERRIES*

Knowing how much you love the sweet juicy taste of fruit, it should come as no surprise to find that other creatures do too. And of them all, the birds are your friendly thieves with the most appetite, least patience, and best timing.

CONGRATULATIONS!
We always knew you
could do it!!

   Birds have secret information as to exactly when the fruit and berries are at their best. Possessed with this knowledge, they sweep down and have a grand feast the moment you turn your back—which is usually about five minutes before you were planning to pick your prize.
   Your warfare with those beloved pests is a pleasant one, fun to see and fun to make. These remedies for pesty birds are "bird foolers." Make them as soon as the fruit is larger than one inch and while your berries are still very tiny. Fool the birds—if you can! Birds are frightened away by windmills (also called pinwheels), bells, silver ribbon,

Fool the birds—if you can!

chimes, and a delightful creature called a dragonfish windsock.

*To Make Bird Foolers*
- Cut long thin strips of aluminum foil and tie these streamers to your tree. When the wind plays with them, the birds won't play with your tree.
- Tie all sorts of delightful sounds to your tree. Old forks and spoons tied to the branches play go-away-bird songs.
- Christmas bells tied to ribbons sway in the breeze and make a nice out of season noise.
- Use small colorful plastic windmills or pinweels, the kind on a stick, sold in the toy section of dime stores. They need only a slight breeze to gaily go round. The movement scares the birds away.

*To Make a Ferocious Dragonfish Windsock*
1. Form a circle with wire three inches across.

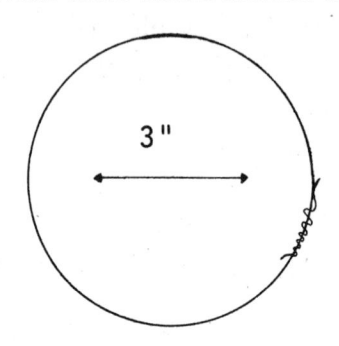

3"

2. Cut a piece of old sheeting 20 inches long by 14 inches wide. Fold in half the long way.

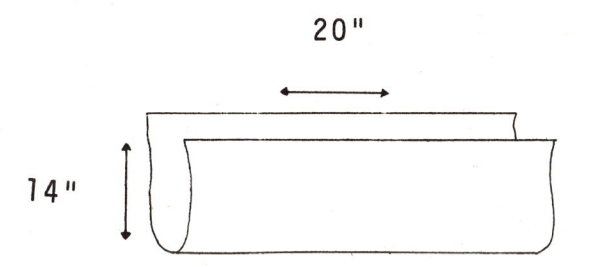

20"

14"

3. Draw an outline of a fish with a nice long tail fin. Cut along the outline. Keep the folded edge as the underbelly and do not cut that part.

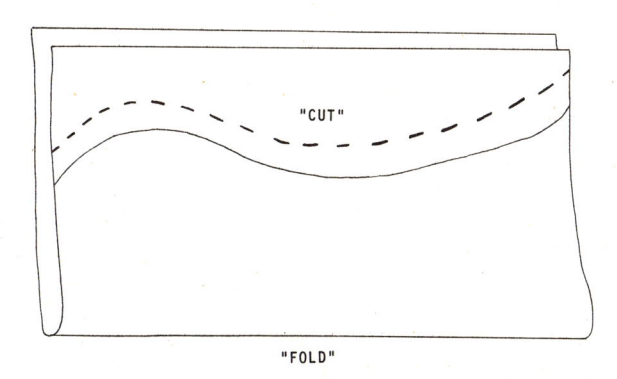

"CUT"

"FOLD"

4. Using crayons or bright paint, color both sides with lots of swirls and wavy fish scales. Add fins and big eyes. Sew the tops together, keeping the mouth and tail sections open.

5. Place the wire circle where the fish's mouth is, and stitch the cloth around the wire to hold it in place. The wire will hold the mouth open.

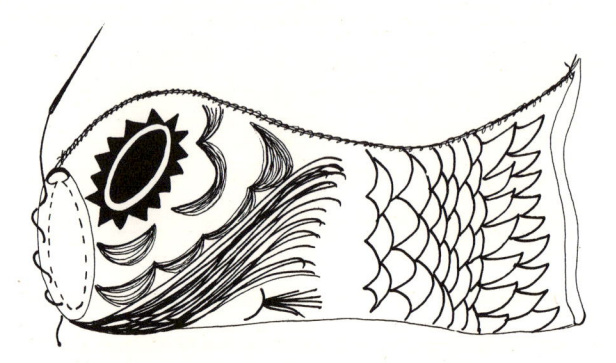

6. Tie your dragonfish windsock to a high outside branch. The wind will blow into the fish's open mouth, keeping the fish ballooned out and ferociously snapping at the birds.

The birds won't even know it's a tree.

*More Remedies*
- Before birds eat grapes and berries, they wait until the fruit has reached just the right dark red ripe color. They stay away from pale colored berries. So try planting some of the delicious golden varieties. While you've had one harvest of fruit after another, the birds will still be waiting for that nice ripe red color that will never come.
- Toss a sheet of cheesecloth, or a bird net, over your fruit trees and berry bushes and forget about the birds. These nets are sold at nurseries, or you can use old lightweight curtains. Nets and curtains will not harm the birds, but will keep them out of the branches and away from the fruit. You of course can reach in anytime.
- Bag your fruits and berries. Slip a small paper bag over the fruit, berries or grapes, and they will be well hidden. The fruit can go on ripening this way. If you use a small plastic bag, make sure you poke some holes through the plastic so cool air can circulate. Otherwise sunlight will collect in this solar heater and you'll harvest stewed fruit. One thing you *shouldn't* do: Do not pick unripe fruit in the hope that you will get it before the birds do. All you will get is a stomach ache!

*The Not-So-Nice Thieves*

Aside from the birds, creepy, crawly, little things like to take their share of your fruit. Keep your tree clean. A thirsty, dusty, little tree offers no resistance to the tiny insects and worms that attack leaves and bark. But a clean, strong tree, which gets regular feeding and watering, gets less bugs and worms.

Noticing things early is the first step. It is easier to get rid of a few pests right away, than after they have completely taken over. Hosing your tree down every once in awhile will help keep bugs off the leaves.

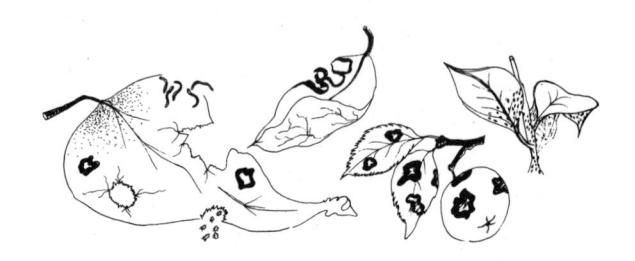

To avoid wormy, deformed fruit, you will have to use an *insecticide* regularly. An insecticide is a powder or spray which kills the insects which eat the fruit. Most insecticides are chemical ones which have unhealthy side effects especially to young children and small animals. For this reason, you should always have an adult spray your trees and bushes. Also be sure to use the least harmful insecticide, one which has an organic base.

Organic insecticides are somewhat safer to use than chemical sprays, because they do not have as bad an effect on the human body. Rotonone, a good spray, is made from organic plant material.

Spray twice a year. Once in late winter or very early spring when the trees are leafless and still in their dormant state, and again in spring after the trees have blossoms.

Senior partners can be helpful.

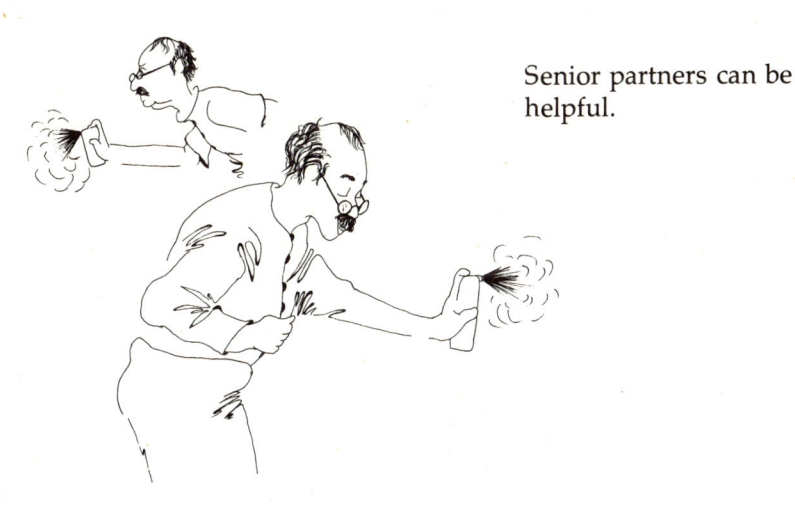

## WINTER

The blossoms have long since faded, the fruit has been harvested, and the leaves have fallen. But fruit trees and berry bushes do not die. Winter will not harm your tree. Asleep for the winter, next spring it will burst into bloom once again, ready for an even bigger and better year. Fruit trees and berry bushes, just like you, get better as they get older.

If you do worry, you can always wrap your tree or bush in a coat of burlap and spread a blanket of mulch on the ground.

*Pruning*

Late winter is pruning season. It is time to begin preparing for the coming summer. You will have to prune some varieties of fruit trees and bushes each year during late January or February, while they are bare and in the dormant state. The tiny genetic dwarfs do not need any pruning, but larger semi-dwarfs do.

*The Living Tree* · 43

Pruning means cutting off some branches entirely and cutting back the remaining ones to shorter lengths. You may wonder why, after all the hard work you and your tree have gone through to grow, should you cut anything off. Pruning will help your tree bear good fruit. If you do not prune your tree, the helpful nutrients will go into making needless long branches, and you will have tiny amounts of small, less meaty fruit. Pruning also keeps the size under control. Without pruning each year, branches will grow farther and farther away from the trunk, and be farther and farther from your reach. The fruit guide at the back of this book will let you know which trees to prune and which wood your particular tree needs to have pruned off.

*The aim of pruning is:*
- To allow all the energy to go to branches that produce fruit instead of to those that do not.
- To make less work for your tree or bush by providing less branches.
- To "clean house" by removing branches so sunlight can reach all the branches, not just the outside tips.
- To keep your tree or bush within a small manageable size.

*General Pruning Guide For Trees*

By the first winter, your tree will have many new branches. They will be whiplike, shiny smooth and reddish in color. The older wood will be a dull grayish color and wrinkled at the point where the new wood begins.

When pruning, use sharp pruning shears. Never tear or break branches.

1. *Thin the Tree.* Remove branches which cross or rub against each other or which are too close to another branch. Check guide at the back of this book to know whether you should cut off the old wood or the new wood. Cut off branches cleanly against the trunk.

2. *Cut Back the Tips of the Remaining Branches.* Larger trees can have the branches cut back by about 1/3 their length, which is usually about 12 inches. For semi-dwarf trees, cut back less. Cut the tips of the branches at an angle, not straight across.

3. *Remove any Suckers or Water Sprouts.* These branches grow from the base of the tree. They are easy to recognize, because they grow

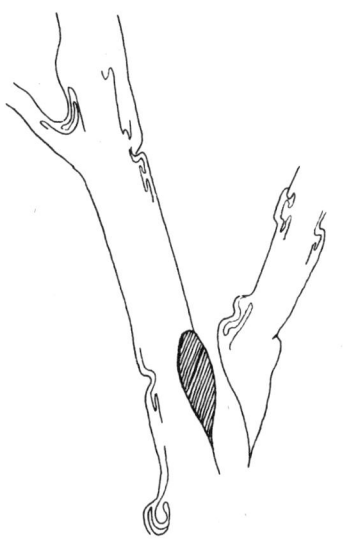

straight up and do not follow the characteristics of the tree. They are useless and use up important energy.

4. *Prune Like an Open Hand.* Keep the desired shape and size of your tree in mind. Trees should have wide open spaces so sunlight can shine between the inside branches.

5. *How to Remember What Wood to Prune.* When your tree finally has fruit, dab some white paint on the branches which bear fruit. On fruit varieties which grow on OLD WOOD, always KEEP the branches which are dabbed white, and each year prune off any others. For fruit varieties which grow on NEW WOOD, CUT OFF the white-dabbed branches. In summer, dab new paint on the branches which bear fruit and at pruning time again remove the white-dabbed

Before pruning.

After pruning.

branches. Each year repeat this to remember the easy way.

Check the fruit guide at the back of the book to see which wood to prune.

*Pruning Guide For Berries*

Berry bushes, especially the berries with thorny canes, need lots and lots of pruning. If they are not heavily pruned, the canes will become thick and tangled briar patches.

Berries which grow on canes live for only one year. The canes die, but the plant lives and produces fresh canes to give you new berries in coming summers. Each year you must cut off the old canes to allow the new ones to grow and produce berries.

1. Cut off at ground level all dry brown berry canes from which you have already harvested berries.
2. New green shoots will be growing at the base of the plant. Choose about four to six of them and cut off their

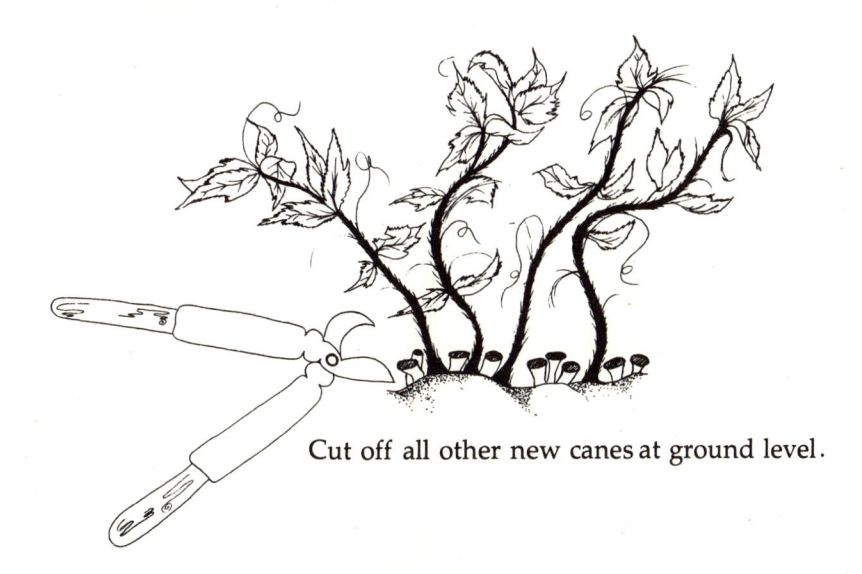

Cut off all other new canes at ground level.

tops so that they are less than 18 inches high. Cut off at ground level all other new green canes.

*Pruning for Pictures*

Especially good in small areas against fences and walls, is the method of pruning which trains a tree to grow the *espaliered* (is-pal-yerd) way. This method flattens out a tree so it will grow upright along a wall or fence—just like a picture. The only branches which are allowed to remain on the tree are those which form right angles to the trunk. These branches are tied to the fence or wall in order to keep that shape permanently. All other branches are cut off. Apple, pear and some plum trees make especially good espaliered trees.

An espaliered tree can grow TREMENDOUS amounts of fruit in a very limited space.

# 4 Fruits and Berries in Pots

Growing fruits and berries in pots gives you FREEDOM. Because potted fruits and berries can be brought indoors when it's cold, you will be free to grow almost any kind of fruit in any kind of climate! And what's more, you will be free to grow your choices anywhere. Dwarf varieties make it possible to have a potted orchard even on the roof. Aside from taking up a little space outside, which must be in the sunshine for six hours a day, the whole secret is in the pot.

Your container must be at least 15 inches wide by 18 inches deep. An 18 by 20-inch container, or even larger sizes, make even better homes. Containers of all sorts can be purchased from a nursery supply store. There are also other kinds you might be able to find for much less money and much more fun. Rummage around in garages, attics, basements, closets and cupboards. Try flea markets and stores. You might even try a gas station, even though it's an unlikely place to look for farm supplies.

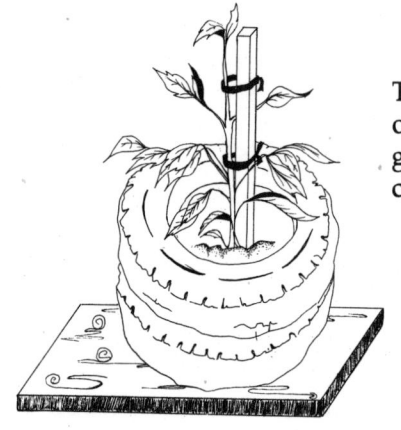

Two or three tires stacked on a wood platform will give you an instant container.

Old oil barrels or gasoline cans can also be used. To remove all traces of harmful chemicals, wash them thoroughly with hot water and strong soap and then rinse in water and vinegar. You can also use:

    half barrels              garbage cans cut in half
    market bushel baskets   old storage bins
    pots and pails           wastebaskets

As you hunt around for a container, you will come up with some very creative ideas for your plants.

**Plant parenthood!**

## TO PLANT ANY FRUIT TREE OR BERRY BUSH IN A POT

1. Purchase a two-cubic foot sack of organic potting soil at your nursery. If you tell the salesperson what you are planting, he or she will sell you just the right type of soil mixture. You will need about one cubic foot of mix for each pot.

*Fruits and Berries in Pots*

2. Clean your container with soap and water, rinse well and dry thoroughly.
3. Make sure there is a hole in the bottom of your container for water to drain through. Place a rock or some broken pieces of crockery over the hole. If you do not have a hole in the container, and you cannot make one, line the bottom of your container with a two-inch layer of pebbles and a two-inch layer of sand over that. This will drain the extra water from the soil just as the hole would have done.
4. Place soil mixture in your pot to a depth of about eight to ten inches. And follow the same directions for planting fruit trees and berry bushes as outlined in Chapter Two.

Plants in containers will need feeding and watering more often than those which are planted in outdoor soil.

## TO WATER

Keep soil moist and cool. But take care not to drown your plants in wet soggy soil. When soil is wet, all the air spaces close up and the plant roots cannot "breathe." When the leaves droop, the plant is not getting enough moisture, and is in soil that is hard and dry. WATER!

## TO FEED

1. Feed your plants every month.
2. Because a potted plant has only a small amount of soil as compared to one growing in the ground, you must

be careful not to let too much of the ingredients in plant food build up in the soil. Too much will hurt the plant. They need a nice balance of soil and food. Therefore, use *half* the amount called for on the label.
3. Use a citrus food.

## WINTER CARE

Potted fruit trees and berry bushes which normally grow in your area are hardy enough to spend winters outdoors, even in very cold climates. If you worry a great deal, it might be a good idea in unusually cold weather to move your pot to a more sheltered location (where there is still sunshine) away from harsh winds.

If you live in a *very cold* climate and are growing a fruit tree that normally grows in a *very warm* climate, like an orange or lemon tree that does not lose its leaves in winter, then you will have to move your pot inside when frost begins to appear. Place the pot near a window where it will get as much sunlight as possible. When spring comes, get your plant used to being outside again by first putting it out in the sunshine during the day only, and bringing it back inside at night. Do this for a week, then your plant will be ready to live outside full time again. When winter comes, put it back inside.

## THE POTTED ORCHARD

Any dwarf tree can be potted. Plant as many in pots as you have room for. Remember to always provide

The potted orchard.

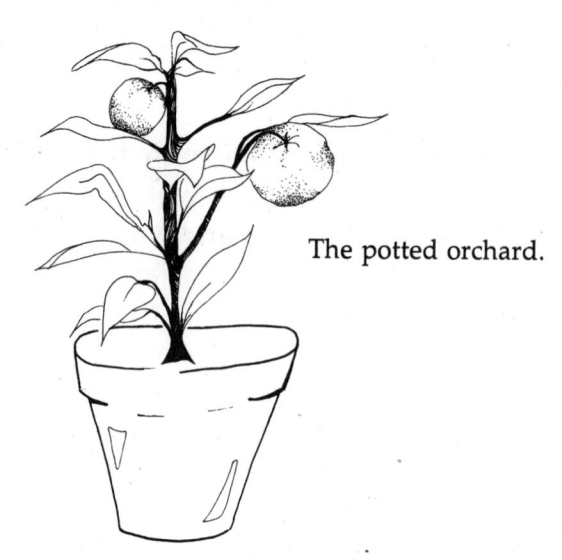

another dwarf variety of your tree to act as a pollinator in order to insure good fruit production.

## GRAPE ARBOR

Use two large pots, about five feet apart, on each side of a doorway, window or gate. You will need two stakes and stiff wire.

Plant one grapevine in each pot. Pound a stake deep into each pot. Nail a wire to the top of each stake. String the wire across the distance you wish covered and fasten to the opposite stake.

As the grapevines grow, tie them up on the stakes. When the vines reach the wire, continue tying them overhead to form the arc and down the stake on the opposite side. Keep the grapevine pruned to this length. If you wish to form a deeper arbor, use four or six pots and line them up behind each other.

If you wish, you can do without the stakes and sim-

Grape arbor.

ply nail wire up along a wall, over a window or door. As the grapevines grow, tie the vines to the wire, framing the door or window.

## STRAWBERRY POTS

Special types of clay pots, ideally suited for growing strawberries, are available at most garden centers. These strawberry pots have little cups popped out along the sides into which you tuck the strawberry plants. The berries grow up, over and all around the pot.

Fill entire pot with soil. Scoop out enough soil to place the strawberry plants into, spreading the roots carefully. Replace soil, firming it all around the plants.

Strawberry pot.

You can also use other kinds of containers to grow strawberries. A shallow flat container makes a good choice. Simply plant your berries all over the top.

### BERRY STICKS

Plant one berry plant in a pot. Hammer a stake deep into the container. As the berry canes grow, twist canes up and around the stake, and presto! you'll have a berry stick to rival any candy stick. Cut off all the canes except for two or three. In larger containers, use two sticks and keep four canes, twisting two canes around each stick.

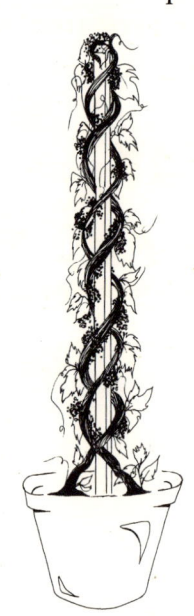

### BLUEBERRY BINS

Blueberry bushes make marvelous container plants. They do not need any support. Just remember to plant two varieties of blueberry bushes in a container, as blueberries are usually self-sterile and need another plant to act as a pollinator so they will bear fruit.

Old crates and bushel baskets make nice roomy containers for more than one blueberry bush. Line the box along the bottom, sides and over the top edge with a sheet of very heavy plastic. You can buy large sheets of plastic at a building supply store or use the largest size garbage can trash bags. This will plant-proof your box by keeping the water and soil from spilling out between the slats or leaky corners.

Blueberry bin.

## THE POTTED PITS

The following plants are all tropicals. Such plants originally developed in warm climates near the equator. They must never be left out in cool or cold weather. Don't get too excited about fruit harvests though, for while you will get a nice green plant, you may not get any fruit. But then again, you may! Either way, you'll get lots of compliments.

*Pineapple*

The first step is to buy a fresh pineapple and eat most of it. The part you save is the top.

*Fruits and Berries in Pots · 57*

1. Cut off the top, leaving less than one inch of pineapple attached to the crown of green leaves. Put this top in a dark place for a few days and allow it to dry out.

2. After two days, place the top of the pineapple in a small pot, about eight inches across, which has been filled with wet sand. Make sure the pineapple portion is well buried in the wet sand.

3. Place the pot in a plastic bag, seal tightly and put where it will get lots of bottom heat. The top of a clothes dryer is usually warm and is a good place. Watch the top carefully and keep the soil moist. It will take several weeks for new green shoots to appear.

4. Once you notice your plant has sprouted, it is time to pot your pineapple in a *larger* container for its permanent home.

5. Gently remove the pineapple top from the wet sand, taking care not to damage any roots. Place the pineapple in a container, filled with potting soil. Bury

the pineapple and leave the crown of leaves well above the soil. Set it in a very warm and sunny spot, always keeping the soil moist.

The outside skin of the pineapple is made up of many little triangle shaped parts. When you see blossoms, you are actually seeing one of the little triangle parts of the pineapple skin. If you don't have any luck with blossoming, try this:

Place a plastic bag over the pineapple plant and put an apple inside, too. Tie the bag tightly so air is trapped inside. After five days, take off the bag. This type of "suffocation" of the pineapple and an apple actually traps a gas mixture given off by the ripening apple which forces the pineapple to flower and form fruit.

When your pineapple is fully developed in size and color with a golden reddish tinge, cut it off. Enjoy eating your harvest. And start all over again.

*The Coffee Bean*

To start a coffee plantation, you can either buy a coffee plant at a nursery, or you can start one from a coffee bean. Many cities have special coffee supply stores where exotic blends of coffee are roasted daily. Go to one of these stores and ask for fresh coffee beans which have NOT YET BEEN ROASTED. Plant these beans in a container filled with potting soil, one to a pot, one inch below the soil line.

A coffee plant likes warm temperatures—over 75 degrees. Once the beans sprout, keep the plants where it is warm and sunny. Do not ever let the soil dry out. Warmth and moist air are what coffee plants like, so spray your plant often. A sunny bathroom is an ideal spot to grow coffee.

Coffee berries are bright crimson. Pick them and remove the skin and flesh. The beans are inside. Place the beans in cool water for a few days until they are smooth to the touch. Then roast them slowly in an oven set on low, until they are dry coffee beans. You can give them to your Mom so she can grind them to brew coffee. Or don't pick the berries at all—just enjoy looking at their bright red color!

# 5 Guide To Growing Individual Fruits and Berries

There are many varieties of each type of fruit or berry from which you may choose. Yellow raspberries or red raspberries? White or purple grapes? Red plums or green ones? Sweet or sour cherries? Some are best eaten fresh, others lend themselves to cooking.

Reading fruit and berry catalogs will help you choose the special varieties best suited to your own taste and your special climate. At the end of this guide is a list of nurseries which will send you colorful fruit and berry catalogs upon request. On rainy days, bring some sunshine inside by deciding which delicious summertime friend you would like to grow.

## APPLE
### *Self-sterile, plant 2 varieties*

Apple trees live a long time, some continuing to bear fruit for as long as 50 years! The original "Delicious" red apple tree sprouted from a seed in 1872. Ten years ago, in Iowa, the tree was still alive and bearing fruit.

Apple trees come in the tiniest size of dwarf all the way up to large standard sized trees. Starkrimson Delicious is a very tiny double dwarf size. Golden Delicious not only comes in the tiny double dwarf size, but it is an exceptionally good pollinator to use with other apple trees. McIntosh is now available in a dwarf size and so is Stark Splendor.

*To Prune*

Apple trees bear their fruit on old wood. Fruit *spurs*,

which are knobby parts that fruit grows on, form on branches, and each year apples are borne on these same fruit spurs. Because apples grow on old wood, less pruning is needed. (The tiny genetic dwarfs need no pruning.) When pruning, just thin out new shiny reddish branches. Cut the remaining old, gray and wrinkled branches back to whatever size you want them to be. Always be careful to save the knobby fruiting spur.

*To remember the easy way.* After your tree has had fruit, dab white paint on those branches which bear apples. Each year, keep these white dabbed branches, pruning off the others.

*To Harvest*

After June, when the apples are very, very tiny, remove some of them so that those left on the branches are a few inches apart. This is called *thinning* the fruit and will help the remaining apples to grow larger.

When picking apples, be careful not to tear fruit spurs, or pull the stems off. Twist or snap the stem off from the spur.

## APRICOT

*Some varieties are self-sterile, plant 2 varieties*

This thousand-year-old fruit, dating back to ancient Chinese cultivation, is one of the prettiest of fruit trees. Moongold and and Sungold are two varieties which MUST always be planted together. Some other varieties may be planted alone and still bear fruit. Moorpark and

Early Golden are two varieties which do well in almost any climate. There are few dwarf varieties, so it would be best to check your local nursery for information as to which, if any, dwarfs will do well in your particular climate.

*To Prune*

Apricots usually grow on *newer* reddish shiny branches which will bear fruit for anywhere from one to three years. Each year, prune off the old grayish wood. Prune the remaining branches so they are well spaced to allow sun to shine inside. Prune also to keep the size tree that you like.

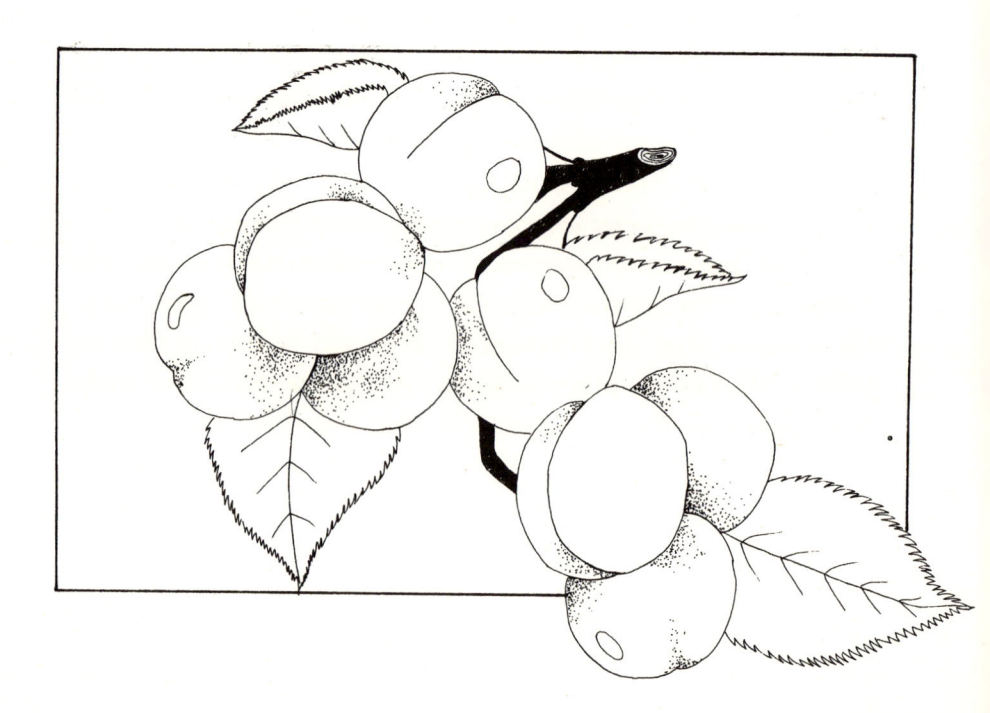

*To remember the easy way.* Dab white paint on the branches that bear apricots. Remove HALF the white-dabbed branches. In the summer, once again dab the branches which bear apricots, and in spring once more remove HALF the white-dabbed branches. Repeat each year.

*To Harvest*

Avoid overcrowding of fruit. When apricots are 3/4 inch in diameter, remove some of them so that the remaining apricots are two to three inches apart. Do not pick the fruit if any green shows. Pick when the color is well developed, but before fruit becomes soft and mushy.

## AVOCADO
### *Self-fertile*

Some people think of avocados as vegetables, but they are definitely a fruit, also known as alligator pears. But no matter what they are called, avocados are a delicious treat.

They need a warm climate, and will grow only where winters are very mild. The trees, which are sold in containers, do not lose their leaves. They grow naturally in a tropical forest where the soil is covered by a heavy blanket of leaves. They like similar soil conditions, so mulch heavily.

Also remember, although trees started from an avocado pit may grow well, they will not bear fruit. You must buy a specific variety of avocado tree in order to grow avocados. Standard sized avocado trees grow very large. These large trees come in two main varieties: Haas and Fuerte. Fuerte has smooth skin and blooms from winter to spring. Haas has a rough, blackish, bumpy skin and grows from spring to summer. The dwarf variety is called Littlecado.

*To Prune*

Avocado trees rarely need pruning except when branches become too low, or when a certain size is desired. Avoid pruning off branches at the top which would create a "hole." The trunks of avocado trees sunburn quite easily and need an overhead canopy of branches. If sun shines through, wrap trunk in strips of cotton to protect it. You can use old sheets, rags, tee shirts—anything you can cut into strips.

*To Harvest*

Pick when a very dark green color and large size is reached. Avocados will continue to ripen even after they have been picked.

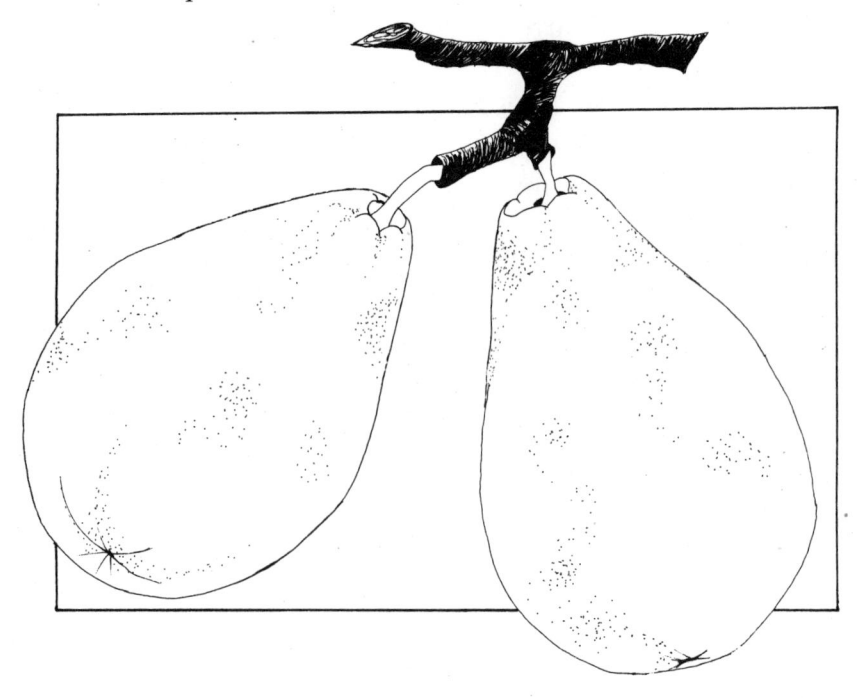

## BLACKBERRY
*Self-fertile*

Blackberries are a rather remarkable family of berries which also include Boysenberries, Loganberries, Dewberries and Youngberries. The different varieties were mostly named after the men who developed each of them. For example, Boysenberry is named in honor of Rudolf Boysen.

Among the world-wide family of blackberries there are at least 100 varieties, or "kissing cousins," from which to choose. Blackberries keep a tiny inside seed core when harvested and are somewhat firm, unlike raspberries which leave their seed core on the stem and are therefore much more fragile. The blackberry is a bramble—a bush, or shrub, with drooping branches covered with little thorns that prick. Of all the brambles, blackberries will root wherever a tip touches the ground and get the most heavily tangled.

Latham is a very popular red variety. Darrow is a good blackberry. Raven is also a good black colored berry.

*To Prune*

*Each year after harvest*, cut off at ground level all the brown dry canes which have produced berries. Choose four to six of the new softer green canes coming up at the base of the plant. Make sure these are four to six inches apart. Trim the tops so they are about 18 inches or less in height. Tie these to your support system. Cut all other canes off at ground level. Prune ruthlessly each year in late fall or early winter.

*To Harvest*

Berries do not keep well and should be eaten right away. Red ones should be all red. Black ones should be nice and dark. They are usually ripe three or four days after turning black.

## BLUEBERRY
*Self-sterile, plant 2 varieties*

These berries are a near relative of the wild but popular huckleberry. Until recently, the blueberry was also considered a wild berry. Fortunately for berry lovers, it is now a domesticated plant that anyone can grow.

Blueberries fall into three types: Highbush which does well in the Eastern United States and grows—you guessed it—high! Good highbush varieties are Eariblue and Berkley. Lowbush blueberries are seldom higher than two feet and can stand cold New England winters well. These are great in containers. Finally, Rabbiteye blueberries of the southern states are a type which do well in warm climate. Callaway and Walker are good rabbiteye varieties. Any two varieties will pollinate each other.

*To Prune*

Blueberry bushes need very little pruning.

1. The side branches are the ones on which the berries grow. Each winter, cut back the tips of the straight branches about six inches and again a few inches in early spring.
2. Keep the blueberry bush from becoming tangled and choked. Remove the old dead tangled branches. If you thin these out, the fruit-bearing ones will have plenty

of room. If you do not have many berries and they are tiny, thin out your branches more. You will get more blueberries and they will be a larger size.

*To Harvest*

Blueberries taste a bit tart until just up to harvest time. Leave them on the bush for one week after they have turned blue. If you pick them immediately after they turn blue, they will taste sour.

## CHERRY
*Self-sterile, plant 2 varieties*

Some varieties of cherry are self-sterile so that you have to plant two different varieties. Others are self-fertile as is the case of the sour cherry tree and may be planted alone. Sour cherries are not really very sour. They are rather tart tasting and are good for cooking and canning. The sour cherry tree is the easiest to grow because it is the least finicky about climate. Sweet cherries are mainly self-sterile and need pollinators. They are the best for eating fresh. The trees are very particular about which ones they will pollinate with.

Plant all cherry trees very early in the spring as they are among the first trees to flower. Stark Gold, a sweet yellow cherry, is a nice, small dwarf tree. Bing is a very popular cherry tree. Both can be pollinated by the Van variety which is a good sweet cherry. Meteor and North Star are both good dwarf varieties of sour cherries which may be planted alone and will still bear fruit. The tiny

Hansen Bush Cherry does well in areas that have extremely cold winters.

*To Prune*

Cherries grow on old gray wrinkled wood. Little knobs and twigs called *fruit spurs* form on wood, and the cherries grow on these little spurs. The spurs continue to bear cherries in the same place year after year. Therefore, cherry trees usually need little pruning. Beyond the first year, pruning is generally done to remove dead or broken branches, and to cut back those branches which grow higher than desired or unwelcome new branches.

*To remember the easy way.* Once your tree bears a full load of cherries, dab white paint on the fruit-bearing branches. At pruning time, keep these white dabbed branches, pruning off the others.

*To Harvest*

Do not yank fruit off the tree— the fruit spurs will be damaged. For eating, pick cherries with the stem on. Cherries for cooking can be picked without the stem. Harvest cherries when they are firm.

## FIG
*Self-sterile, plant 2 varieties*

The fig is really an inside-out flower. The skin is on the outside. Inside are the many tiny little petals which make up the fig meat. Fig trees are considered a warm-climate tree. Some varieties will bear fruit in the milder areas of the northwest, but the trees will be very small and more like a bush. In the heat of the west or southwest, the fig tree may grow as large as 25 feet. There is no dwarf variety, but the tree may be kept very small by a lot of pruning.

*To Prune*

Different varieties of figs require different pruning techniques. White and brown figs grow on shiny reddish new wood. All the previous year's wood should be cut back so the tree just has a few stubs. Nothing more! Black varieties grow on old gray wrinkled wood. These types of fig trees need only be pruned in order to keep whatever size and shape you wish.

*To Harvest*

Figs grow straight up. They should not be picked until the necks shrivel and the fruit hang straight down. If white sap appears after a fruit is picked, it means it has been picked too soon. For dried figs, allow figs to fall from the tree and finish drying them on a tray in the sun.

## GRAPES
*Self-fertile*

Grapes do better in poor soil than any other fruit. They actually account for one-fourth of all the fruit produced commercially in the entire world. Most grapes are used to make wine.

Grapes come in many, many varieties, ranging in color from purplish black to green to pearly white. No matter which variety you choose to grow, plan to trail the vines along a wall, fence or stake. Grapes like to go up and then hang down. Great for arbors along fences and walls. Grapes can also be grown in deep pots. Check with your local nursery to find out which variety grows best in your area. Buffalo and Concord are excellent blue-black grapes. Thompson Seedless is a golden-green seedless grape and makes good raisins.

*To Prune*

*First Summer.*

1. Allow the plant to grow a number of branches. Select a strong center branch for a main "trunk" and four well spaced strong branches to form the side arms.
2. Tie the center branch to a straight stake.
3. Tie the side branches along wire stretched to each side or to other supports.
4. Cut off all other branches.

*Each year thereafter.* Remove branches which have borne grapes and turned old, gray and woody. Keep the center "trunk" clear of any branches except the four side arms, and their smooth new shiny branches which will bear fresh grapes next year.

*To remember the easy way.* Dab some white paint on the grape-bearing branches. At pruning time, cut off the white dabbed branches above where the trunk and four side-arm spread begins. In summer, once again dab white paint on grape-bearing branches in order to know which branches need pruning off in the winter. Repeat each year.

*To Harvest*

Always pick a grape from the tip of the bunch to taste-test for harvest. Pick the rest when your taste-test tells you the grapes are sweet.

## GRAPEFRUIT
### *Self-fertile*

A member of the citrus family, grapefruits come in white and red flesh varieties. In order to manufacture sweet fruit, the trees must grow only where desert heat is available. Grapefruit trees are available in standard and dwarf sizes. The dwarf grapefruit sometimes does well even if it is not grown in its ideal warm climate. In cold areas, the fruit is thick skinned and not very good, but the tree is very pretty and decorative, even when the fruit is poor. Grapefruit trees bloom with thousands of very fragrant blossoms! They keep their leaves year round. Marsh

is a good white grapefruit and Ruby a popular red one.
*To Prune*

Grapefruit trees do not need regular pruning. Prune only at planting time so that permanent branches can be shaped. Keeping the tree at a certain size, however, may require cutting back some of the new branches. Beware—some branches are very thorny.

Grapefruit trees are always sold in containers, never bare-root.

*To Harvest*

Allow grapefruit to ripen on the tree. When ready, cut off just a tiny bit above where the stem joins the fruit.

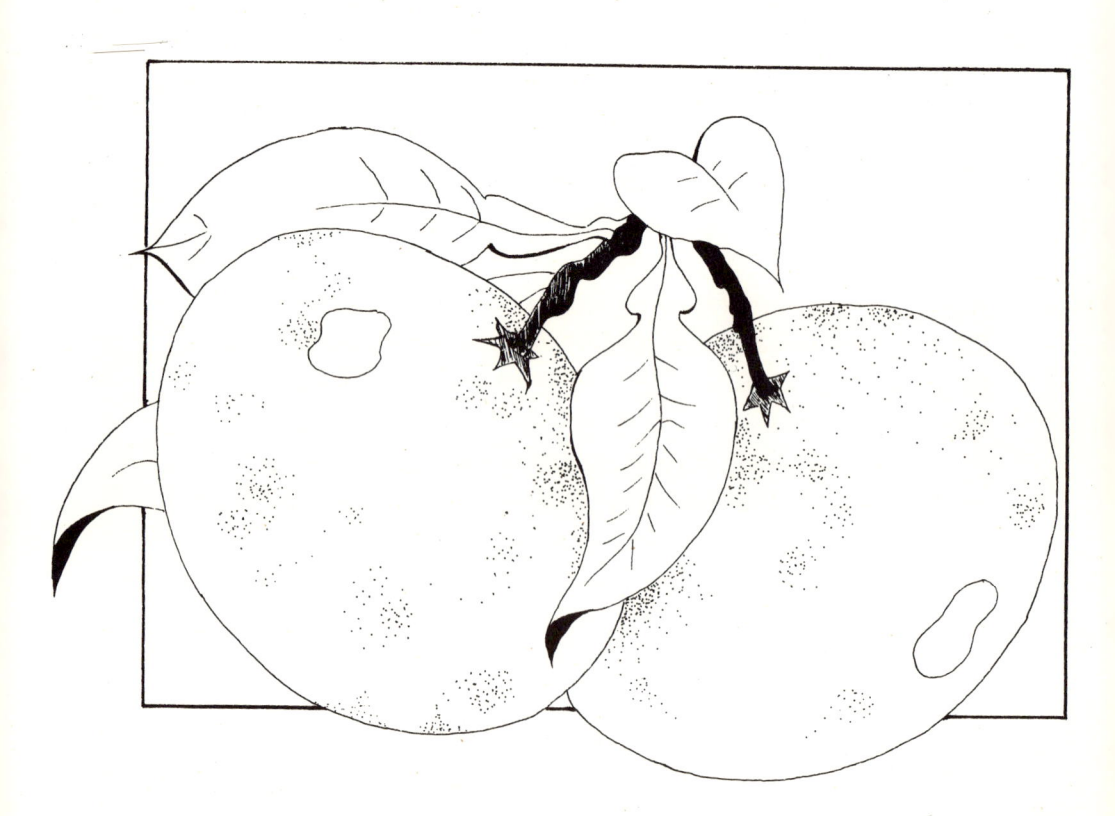

## LEMONS AND LIMES
*Self-fertile*

Members of the citrus family, these trees never lose their leaves. Lemons have a bright yellow skin. Limes are green. Lemons do not like too much heat. They grow nicely in coastal areas or mild northern areas with no frost. Limes need even milder winters, and they really like high heat. Lemon and lime trees are always sold in containers.

Lemons are a favorite of indoor gardeners. Even some of the tiniest varieties of dwarf trees bear giant fruit. Where winters are harsh, the tiny trees can be potted and taken indoors. The fragrant blossoms and shiny green leaves make them a delightful house plant. Eureka is a really tiny lemon "bush" which produces big lemons. The "bush" can be shaped into a tiny tree by pruning off the extra branches. Meyer is another very tiny dwarf lemon tree.

*To Prune*

The first pruning is done so branches can face in all directions and be evenly spaced around the trunk. Thereafter, pruning need only be done to remove crowded, or dead branches, and generally just to help keep the shape and size of the tree as you like it.

*To Harvest*

Harvest when full color is reached. Cut a little above where the stem joins the fruit.

## NECTARINE. See Peach.

## ORANGE
*Self-fertile*

Oranges are a citrus fruit. The trees keep their leaves year round. Mandarin Orange, Tangerine, and Tangelo are all members of the orange family. They are beautiful to look at and have very fragrant blossoms. Since orange trees are susceptible to cold, they need summer and winter heat to develop sweetness. Dwarf varieties make it possible to grow them as potted plants where climates are cold. Orange trees are sold in containers, not bare-root. The best time to plant is in very early spring, before the blossoms appear.

Valencia oranges are usually better for juice, and Navel are good for eating. Both are available in dwarf varieties. Mineola Tangelo is the name of a dwarf variety which is a combination of orange and tangerine.

*To Prune*

Aside from pruning at planting time to help form the permanent shape of the tree, orange trees need very little pruning. Any pruning which is done should mainly be to remove any dead, old, crowded and broken branches and to keep the shape of the tree the way that you like it.

*To Harvest*

Pick oranges when color is well developed and there is not a trace of green left upon them. Snip the stem a little above where it joins the fruit.

## PEACH AND NECTARINE
*Most varieties self-fertile*

Peaches and nectarines, being so alike, are grouped together here. It is entirely possible that one branch of a peach tree may suddenly begin producing a fuzzless peach—a nectarine—and vice versa! Peaches are a favorite with home gardeners. Not only does the sweet and juicy fruit taste good, but there are also so many of them to harvest.

Varieties are available for almost any climate. Check with the nursery people when you make your purchase. Bonanza and Stark Starlet are two very good and tiny dwarf peach varieties. Reliance is a peach tree that does well even where winters dip below zero. Nectarina is a very tiny variety of nectarine tree.

*To Prune*

Tiny genetic dwarfs do not need to be pruned. The larger semi-dwarfs need pruning. Because most peaches grow on new wood, pruning a fruit tree heavily will encourage new growth and insure a steady supply of peaches.

Remove all the old grayish colored wood and any crowded branches. Prune branches so the remaining new reddish shiny ones are well spaced. After this thinning, cut back the tips of the remaining branches. You can cut as much as one-third off the length of the branch. By pruning back very much, you will encourage lots of new wood and still keep your peaches within easy reach. The same pruning, perhaps a bit less, is necessary for nectarine trees.

*Remembering the easy way.* Dab some white paint on the branches which have peaches on them. At pruning time, simply cut off these white-marked branches. In summertime, once again dab paint on the fruit bearing branches and at pruning time, cut those off.

*To Harvest*

When there is not a trace of green, gently twist the fruit. Do not press as peaches and nectarines bruise easily. If it gives way easily, you have chosen just the right moment! Using your pruning shears to cut the fruit stem just below where it joins the tree, may make harvesting easier.

## PEAR
### *Self-sterile, plant 2 varieties*

Pear trees are somewhat fussy about where they grow. They do not like too much heat or too much cold. Aside from the apple tree, the pear tree lends itself most easily to espaliering and to shapes suited for small areas.

Dwarf varieties are available. Duchess is a variety which is self-pollinating, but will pollinate other varieties. It happens to do best as a dwarf. Keiffer is a variety which grows well almost anywhere. Starkling Delicious is the name of a very nice dwarf tree. Bartlett, the best known pear in the United States, also comes in dwarf size.

*To Prune*

Pear trees bear their fruit on fruit spurs. These knobby little spurs are located on old gray wood, so pear trees need very little pruning, just enough to keep it the size and shape you like. Prune when planting. After that, prune to remove old, broken or dead branches, and shiny reddish branches which crowd the tree. Cut back branches that get too high.

*To remember the easy way.* Dab white paint on the branches which have pears and keep these paint-dabbed branches. Prune off all others.

To Harvest

Pears, unlike any other fruits, do not ripen on the tree! They must be harvested BEFORE they are ripe—while they are still green—or they will spoil. Pick pears when they have reached full size, but are still green. Once you notice any yellow, harvest in a hurry!

To remove from tree, pull gently in an upwards direction. Be careful not to damage the fruit spur, the little knobby part where the pear stem attaches itself to the tree. Using your pruning shears to cut the fruit stem just below where it joins the tree, may make harvesting easier. Pears bruise very easily, so take care not to drop or handle them roughly. Store in a cool dark place such as a basement or refrigerator. Remove from storage about a week before you want to use them. To ripen pears quickly, place several together inside a paper bag in a warm room.

## PLUM
### *Self-sterile, plant 2 varieties*

Plums come in European, American and Oriental varieties. Orientals are generally red, European are bluish and American plums are mainly red with some yellow. Because of the many varieties, you can be sure of a plum tree to suit your climate and your taste. Did you know that a plum is a fresh prune, and a prune is a sundried plum?

The dwarf Santa Rosa is a great plum and a very good pollinizer for other varieties of plum trees. Damson is a small tree, and some nurseries offer it as a dwarf. It is self-pollinating and makes terrific jam. Starkling Delicious is a very hardy plum tree with ruby red fruit. Stanley Prune is a popular purple plum, and its plums make—you guessed it—good prunes.

*To Prune*

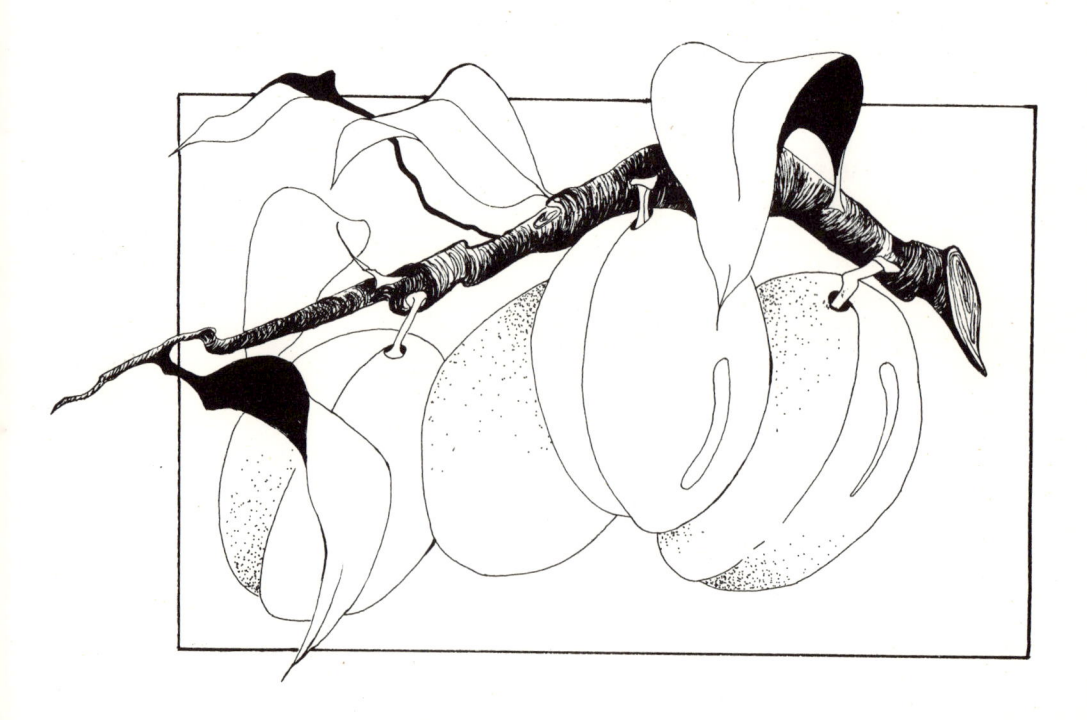

Fruit forms on fruit spurs, which develop on old grayish wrinkled wood. Keep the old wood. Each year, prune out those new shiny reddish colored branches in order to keep the limbs or branches well spaced so sunlight can enter the tree. Remove dead and broken branches. Cut back the tips of the remaining branches 1/3 of the length of the branch.

*To remember the easy way.* Dab white paint on those branches bearing plums and keep those branches. Prune off the others.

To Harvest

Plums should be picked when their color is well developed and there is no trace of green. They should be firm to the touch, not hard. If you like riper plums, pick them when they are somewhat softer to the touch.

Using your pruning shears to cut the fruit stem just below where it joins the tree, may make harvesting easier.

Prunes are made by allowing plums to become overripe and drop from the tree. These are then spread on a tray to continue drying out in the sun.

## RASPBERRY
### Self-fertile

Because these berries are so fragile, they are not usually available in large quantities in supermarkets and so are very costly. Because raspberries are so hard to find, they are a special delight to home gardeners.

Raspberries are different from all other berries. When they are harvested, they leave their inside seed on the cane. The berry pulls free of this inner core, and becomes a very soft hollowed-out fruit! This is the reason why it's so fragile.

Raspberries come in eye-catching colors of purple, black, red and yellow. The birds like the dark ones best, and tend to leave the yellow ones alone. Canby is a very good thornless red raspberry. Latham is a dependable red berry which is very hardy even in very cold climates. Black Hawk is a good black raspberry, and Bodus is a nice big purple one. September is a good red "everbearer" which will give you two crops each year. Amber and Golden West are two varieties of golden colored raspberries.

*To Prune*

*Each year after harvest time.* Cut off at ground level all the dry brown canes which have produced berries. These will not produce berries again. Choose four to six of the newest soft green canes coming up at the base of the plant. Be sure they are four to six inches apart, and cut them so they are no higher than 18 inches off the ground. Tie up these new canes in a tepee style or to your support system. They will give you berries next year. If you allow too many canes to grow, you'll have loads of canes and hardly any berries. Cut off all other canes at ground level.

*To Harvest*

Pull off when color is just right and the berries are no longer hard. Pick berries gently with just two fingers and cup them in the palm of your hand. Do not heap into a pile or the berries will bruise. The darker colored berries will be ready for picking three or four days after they turn purple or black. Do not wash raspberries until just before you are ready to eat them as washing makes this fragile berry spoil even faster.

## STRAWBERRIES
### *Self-fertile*

Strawberries are the most widely grown fruit of the home gardener. And they have the shortest span of life of all the fruits and berries. Strawberry plants must be dug up and replaced after three years.

Strawberries are sold as little plants in a tray or box. These can be grown very easily in the soil or in shallow pots or pans (*See* Chapter 4). Strawberries grown in the ground love mulch. Since the berries lie on the soil, the mulch will protect them from decay.

Ozark Beauty is a very popular variety and is stocked in almost every nursery. Shasta grows well in California.

Florida 90 is good for southern gulf coasts. Surecrop is a very vigorous and hardy strawberry.

*To Plant*

Prepare an outdoor strawberry patch by spading up the ground. Remove all ground cover and loosen the soil. For a patch four feet by six feet, you will need a two-cubic-foot bag of planter mix. Dig the planter mix into the patch, mixing it with the soil to a depth of about six inches.

Dig small holes eight to twelve inches apart for your strawberry plants. Set them into the holes so that one half of the root crown is below ground and one half above ground. The crown is the portion of the plant where the stem and the roots meet. Press the soil firmly around the plants.

Each strawberry plant will send out several stems called *runners*. These runners will put down roots and form new plants wherever they touch the ground. Because of this, it is very difficult to keep strawberry plants in neat rows. It is much easier to just plant the strawberries at random all over the patch and let the runners take root wherever they want. Then you can just keep the outside edge of the strawberry patch from spreading, and let the inside of your patch fill with berries.

*To Prune*

Allow 12 inches on the outside of your strawberry patch for the runners to spread. Anything beyond those 12 inches should be snipped off. Strawberries inside the patch will need cleaning more than pruning. Rummage around the leaves and remove dead leaves and berries that have fallen to the ground.

*To Harvest*

Jerk the stem off, or simply pinch the stem and twist. Do not pull on the berry. If you pull on the berry itself, you will end up pulling the berry off without the little green cap. Berries without these stem caps spoil very quickly and must be eaten right away.

TANGERINE. *See Orange.*

## WHERE TO ORDER FRUITS AND BERRIES

Strybling Nurseries
P.O. Box 793
Merced, CA 95340

Armstrong Nursery
1265 S. Palmetto Avenue
Ontario, CA 91761

W. Atlee Burpee Co.
P.O. Box 748
Riverside, CA 92502

H. G. Hastings
P.O. Box 44088
Atlanta, GA 30336

R. H. Shumway Seedsman
Rockford, IL 61101

Henry Field Seed & Nursery Co.
Shenandoah, Iowa 51602

Bountiful Ridge Nurseries, Inc.
Princess Anne, MD 21853

Burgess Seed and Plant Co.
P.O. Box 3001
Galesburg, MI 49053

Farmer Seed and Nursery Co.
Fairbault, MN 55021

Stark Bros. Nursery
Louisiana, MO 73353

Henry Leuthardt Nurseries, Inc.
East Moriches,
Long Island, N.Y. 11940

Gurneys Seed & Nursery Co.
Yankton, S.D. 57078

Van Well Nursery
P.O. Box 1339
Wenatchee, WA 98801

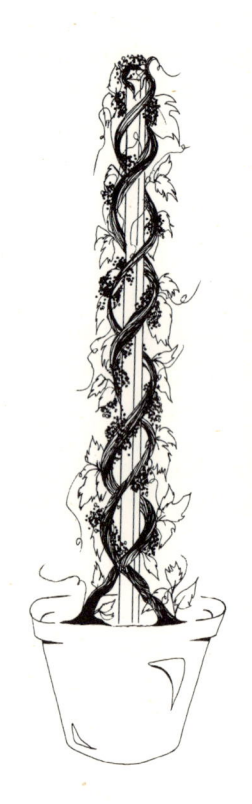

# GLOSSARY

**Alligator pear**—Another name for an avocado.

**Bare-root tree**—A tree whose roots are free of soil. It is the way many trees and bushes are sold by plant nurseries.

**Bramble**—A rough or prickly bush or vine. This is also a popular name for Blackberries and related berries, such as Dewberries, Boysenberries and Loganberries.

**Bud union**—The bump in a tree where it was grafted.

**Bushes**—Fully grown plants that are less than about 15 feet high, and have a dense thicket of branches, and very often found growing in clumps that look like a single plant.

**Cane**—The stalk or trunk of some berry plants. They bend easily and have to be supported on wires or stakes.

**Carbon dioxide**—A chemical, usually found in the form of a gas or vapor, like the air around us, which actually contains a lot of carbon dioxide. It is one of the ingredients a plant uses to make sugar.

**Dormant**—Another word for "not growing" or "inactive," but still alive.

**Espalier**—A plant that is trained to grow flat against a support such as a wall or trellis.

**Fertilize**—The process of making a plant ready to bear fruit.

**Fertilizer**—Any substance such as a chemical or manure which will supply plants with some or all of their food needs. The term, as used in this sense, is not related to the word "fertilize" defined above.

**Fruit spur**—A knobby growth or bump on a twig or small branch. It is the place on fruit trees where the fruit develops.

**Genetic dwarf**—A tree that grows naturally small, without any human interference.

**Grafting**—The process of cutting the top off one type of tree or plant and bandaging it on to the bottom part of another type.

**Insecticide**—A chemical spray, liquid or powder which kills insects but is not supposed to hurt plants, animals or humans. But a lot of people differ about this.

**Irrigation**—The process of adding water to a field or garden when the rainfall is not enough or is delayed by a drought.

**Mulch**—Any material such as sawdust, leaves, or old newspaper which is laid on the ground around the roots of plants to protect them from very hot or very cold weather.

**New wood**—Refers to the new stems and twigs that grow each year on a fruit tree.

**Nitrogen**—A chemical, usually found in the air as a gas or vapor. It is one of the essential foods of plants.

**Phosphorous**—A yellow, waxy chemical that glows in the dark, burns at room temperature. It is never seen in its pure form for that reason, but is always mixed with some other substance to form a whitish rock called phosphate. In this form it is a main food for plants.

**Pollen**—The powderlike substance that is the male plant fertilizing material, and must be dusted on to the flower of another plant before that plant can bear fruit.

**Pollinate**—To fertilize by pollen; *see also* Fertilize; Pollen.

**Potassium**—A silver-white metal which has the "magic" power to burn water, but is never seen in its pure form outside the chemical laboratory (it is explosive). However, combined in fertilizers, it is a main food for plants.

**Pruning**—Cutting back the branches of a tree or plant. Pruning helps plants recover from the shock of being moved, and helps them to bear more and better fruit.

**Rootstock**—The bottom part of a tree to which the top of another tree is to be grafted.

**Self-fertile**—The condition of a plant that is able to fertilize itself, without the pollen of another plant.

**Self-sterile**—A condition of a plant that cannot fertilize itself, but needs the pollen of another variety of that plant in order to bear fruit. *See* variety.

**Shrub**—A spreading woody plant with many stems that branch out at or near ground level. It is usually less than about ten feet high.

**Sterile**—A condition in which a plant is unable to bear fruit—that is, it cannot have off-spring.

**Trellis**—A frame made from interlaced or criss-crossed slats of wood or metal, and used as a support for plants.

**Variety**—A plant of one type which is slightly different from others of that same type.

# INDEX

alligator pears. *See* avocado
apples, 9, 48, 59, 63; Golden Delicious, 62; McIntosh, 62; Starkrimson Delicious, 62; Stark Splendor, 62
apple trees, 62, 82
apricot, 63–65; Early Golden, 64; Moongold, 63; Moorpark, 63; Sungold, 63
avocado, 65–66; Fuerte, 65–66; Haas, 65–66; Littlecado, 66

bare-root berries, 28
bare-root bush, 22, 29
bare-root trees, 22, 24, 25, 78
bees, 18
berries, 9, 10, 21, 22, 27, 28, 30, 34, 35, 36, 37, 41, 47, 49, 53, 55, 56, 60, 61, 67, 68, 70, 85, 86, 87, 89. *See also* individual names
bird foolers, 37–41
birds, 36–37, 41, 86
blackberry, 67–68; Darrow, 68; Latham, 68; Raven, 68
blossoms, 16, 18, 32, 42, 43, 59, 76, 77, 78
blueberry, 56, 68–70; Berkley, 69; Callaway, 69; Eariblue, 68; Highbush, 68; Lowbush, 69; Rabbiteye, 69; Walker, 69

Boysen, Rudolph, 67
Boysenberries, 67
bramble, 28, 67, 68
bud union, 14
bush, 9, 15–16, 21, 22, 23, 24, 27, 29, 30, 32, 34, 35, 36, 41, 42, 43, 44, 47, 52, 67, 72, 77, 78

California, 87
cane fruits, 28
canes, 28, 30, 47, 48, 56, 68, 85, 86, 87
canned berries, 28
canned trees, 23, 24, 25
carbon dioxide, 35
chemical sprays, 42
cherries, 61, 70–72; Bing, 70; Hansen Bush, 71; Meteor, 70; North Star, 70; Stark Gold, 70; Van, 70
Chinese, 63
citrus, 21, 23, 75, 77, 78
citrus fertilizer, 35
citrus food, 20, 35, 53
climate, 15, 16, 21, 49, 53, 57, 61, 64, 65, 69, 70, 72, 75, 77, 78, 80, 84, 86
coffee bean, 59, 60
coffee berries, 60
coffee plantation, 59

companion tree, 16–18

Dewberries, 67
dormant, 21, 43
dwarfs, 12, 13, 14, 16, 24, 33, 49, 53–54, 62, 64, 66, 70, 72, 77, 78, 79, 80, 82, 84

espaliered trees, 48, 82

fertile, 16
fertilization, 18
fig, 72–73
fruit, 9, 10, 12, 13, 14, 15, 16, 18, 21, 22, 26, 32, 34, 35, 36, 37, 41, 42, 43, 44, 46, 49, 54, 56, 57, 59, 61, 62, 63, 64, 65, 70, 72, 73, 75, 76, 77, 78, 79, 80, 81, 82, 83, 84, 85, 87 See also individual names
fruit spurs, 62–63, 71, 72, 82, 83, 84

gardeners, 13, 77, 80, 85, 87
genetic dwarfs, 13, 43, 63, 81
graft, 14
grafting, 13
grapefruit, 75–76; Marsh, 76; Ruby, 76
grapes, 28, 41, 61, 73–75; Buffalo, 74; Concord, 74; Thompson Seedless, 74
grapevine, 54–55

harvest, 57, 63, 65, 66, 67, 68, 70, 72, 73, 75, 76, 78, 79, 80, 83, 85, 87, 89
Starkling Delicious, 82

huckleberry, 68

insecticide, 20, 42
insects, 41–42
Iowa, 62
irrigation, 32

lemon, 53, 77–78; Eureka, 77; Meyer, 78
lime, 77
Loganberries, 67

mail-order catalogs, 21, 61, 90
Mineola Tangerine, 79
mulch, 34, 35, 43, 65, 87
mulching, 34

nectar, 18
Nectarina, 81
nectarine. See peach
New England, 69
nitrogen, 35–36
nurseries, 14, 15, 21, 22, 41, 61, 84
nursery, 15, 18, 23, 34, 35, 49, 51, 59, 64, 74, 80, 87

orange, 53, 78–79; Mandarin, 78; Navel, 79; Valencia, 79
orchard, 10, 16, 49
organic potting soil, 51, 58, 59

patches, 10, 12, 28, 47, 88, 89
peaches, 9, 80–81; Alberta, 18; Bonanza, 80; Freestone, 18; Stark Starlet, 80
pear, 48, 81, 82–83; Bartlett, 82; Duchess, 82; Keiffer, 82;
phosphorous, 35–36

pineapple, 16, 57–59
plant food, 35, 36
planter mix, 20, 24, 28, 88
plum, 48, 61, 81, 83–85; American, 83–84; Damson, 84; European, 83–84; Oriental, 83–84; Santa Rosa, 84; Stanley Prune, 84; Starkling Delicious, 84
pollen, 16, 18
pollinator, 18, 54, 56, 62, 70
pollinization, 16
pot, 16, 49, 52, 53, 54, 55, 56, 58, 59, 74, 78, 87
potassium, 35–36
prune, 84
pruning, 26, 30, 43, 44, 45, 46, 47, 48, 54, 62, 63, 64, 66, 68, 69, 71, 72, 74–75, 76, 78, 79, 81, 83, 84–85, 86, 89
pruning season, 43, 46
pruning shears, 20, 25, 45

raspberries, 61, 67, 85–87; American, 86; Bodus, 86; Canby, 86; Golden West, 86; Latham, 86; September, 86
roots, 14, 21, 22, 25, 26, 34, 36, 52, 55, 58, 67, 88, 89
rootstock, 13, 14
Rotonone. *See* insecticide
runners, 89

self-fertile, 18, 70, 73, 77, 78, 80, 85, 87
self-pollinating, 82, 84
self-sterile, 16, 56, 62, 70, 72, 82, 84

semi-dwarf, 14–15, 24, 43, 45, 81
soil, 14, 20, 22, 23, 24, 25, 26, 27, 28, 33, 34, 36, 52, 53, 55, 58, 59, 60, 65, 73, 87, 88
soil mixture, 25, 29, 51–52
stakes, 20, 27, 28, 30, 54, 56, 73, 74
standard size trees, 10, 12, 13, 24, 34, 62, 65
sterile, 16
strawberries, 55, 56, 87–89; Florida 90, 88; Ozark Beauty, 87; Shasta, 87

Tangelo, 78
Tangerine, 78
topsoil, 33
tree, 9, 12, 13, 14, 15, 16, 18, 21, 22, 23, 24, 25, 26, 27, 32, 33, 34, 35, 36, 41, 42, 43, 44, 45, 46, 48, 52, 53, 54, 62, 63, 64, 65, 70, 71, 72, 75, 76, 77, 78, 79, 83, 84, 85
tropicals, 57

United States, 68, 82

varieties, 15, 18, 46, 49, 61, 62, 63, 64, 65, 67, 68, 69, 70, 72, 73, 75, 78, 79, 80, 82, 83, 84
variety, 13, 16, 18, 54, 65, 66, 68, 70, 72, 73, 81, 86, 87
vines, 28, 30, 54, 73

water, 25, 26, 32, 33, 34, 35, 36, 41–42, 52

Youngberries, 67